THE AGEING PARENT HANDBOOK 1994

'Be comfort to my age!'

William Shakespeare, *As You Like It*

Let me grow lovely, growing old –
So many fine things to do.
Laces and ivory and gold
And silks need not be new;
And there is healing in old trees;
Old streets a glamour hold;
Why may not I, as well as these,
Grow lovely, growing old?

Karl Wilson Baker (b.1878)

'You are old, Father William,' the young man said,
'And your hair has become very white;
And yet you incessantly stand on your head –
Do you think, at your age, it is right?'

Lewis Carroll (1832–1898)

THE
AGEING PARENT HANDBOOK
1994

*The directory of everything you need to know
as relatives and friends grow older*

BELINDA HADDEN

Thorsons
An Imprint of HarperCollins*Publishers*

Thorsons
An Imprint of HarperCollinsPublishers
77–85 Fulham Palace Road,
Hammersmith, London W6 8JB

Published by Thorsons 1994
1 3 5 7 9 10 8 6 4 2

A catalogue record for this book
is available from the British Library

ISBN 0 7225 2952 X

Printed in Great Britain by
Mackays of Chatham, Kent

*To all my friends, and the people I met who told me
'I wish we'd had this book when we needed it!'*

CONTENTS

FOREWORD

THE URGENT CHALLENGE presented by Britain's fast-growing older population makes *The Ageing Parent Handbook 1994* highly topical and long overdue.

Today's ageing population is the baby boomer generation's responsibility and, although we don't have the extended family tradition that is the norm in fellow European countries, we mustn't shirk our obligations nor offload them.

Personally I have awesomely energetic and fit parents in their late sixties and seventies. Legally, old age may be anything over 50 but my mother didn't become Prime Minister until she was 54 and the inquiry I recall fielding most often was for the secret of her stamina—usually by someone years her junior!

So I read *The Ageing Parent Handbook 1994* with 'L' plates on as far as any first-hand experience of the phenomenon went. I couldn't even complete the questionnaire on page 17.

Considering the plethora of literature available on childhood, adolescence, the mid-life crisis and myriad other hurdles between cradle and grave, it is extraordinary that there is so little published to smooth the path through the pitfall years at the tail end of our lifespan.

The first tangible reminder of a parent or elderly relative's mortality—whether sudden or gradual—often triggers complete panic in the next of kin as they face up to their and the relation's changed circumstances. It is a whole new scene and a daunting one as to what to do, how to find out about the choices and which expert organisations to turn to.

I am sure this book will help transform the nation's attitude to old age to a far more pragmatic and positive one. It is an admirably comprehensive guide through the snakes and ladders of old age. It is compulsory reading before any family summit which is going to decide what's best for granny or grandpa once life is no longer the sunlit bliss portrayed in television adverts for this or that retirement plan or home.

The Ageing Parent Handbook 1994 is a reference book, a comfort, an inspiration and an ally which will enable older people and their children to make the right mutually beneficial decisions, together. I wish I'd written it because every family needs a copy!

Carol Thatcher
September 1993

INTRODUCTION

ALTHOUGH SHE WON'T THANK ME for pointing it out, my aunt is 81 this year. She has lived alone for 20 years in a London flat. Many of her friends have died, she fell out with her daughter over a decade ago, and she is my responsibility. There is no one else.

It was this last point which proved the inspiration for this book. I needed a handbook, a compendium or a single-source directory of all the public and private organisations that exist to help in this area, many of whose individual leaflets I'd seen in my local library. I couldn't seem to find one. I went to the library—nothing.

There were books, of course: on old age; coping with old age, adjusting to old age, on services for older people, even caring for your parents. But there appeared to be nothing written for younger people, telling them the options on all the issues and listing all the organisations that can help and advise people in my position.

Perhaps this is because old age is not a glamorous subject. Perhaps families who resort to dumping or abusing their older relatives might benefit if they knew what help is available (often just for the price of a stamped addressed envelope) from the many hundreds of commercial and charitable organisations all over the UK whom we have identified and included in this book.

As medical breakthroughs continue and healthier lifestyles prolong lives, more families just like mine are going to need to plan their relatives' futures. Older people are an important group—28 members of parliament list 'older people' as their special interest—and growing old is a prospect that we all face sooner or later. It seemed high time that someone wrote such a book. And so it was that I decided to do so.

Having never written a book before it has taken me a good deal of time to research and write it. However, I have been greatly encouraged by the response from people of my age to whom I have spoken—many of whom have asked for a copy. I have been able to pass on advice to friends with elderly relatives on a number of subjects along the way.

I have been greatly assisted by my husband and our great friend Julian Grazebrook who, as an accountant, has researched, checked and drafted all the financial and legal details. Incidentally, while I hope you find these sections informative, you should always seek the advice of a professional before making a commitment.

Leaving aside the enormity of the task and the fascination my computer held for my two-year-old daughter Camilla, perhaps the greatest problem in putting together this book was finding the right title for it. After months of discussion we came up with the somewhat functional-sounding *The Ageing Parent Handbook 1994: the directory of everything you need to know as relatives and friends grow older.*

As we prepared to dispatch nearly 800 'topped and tailed' letters to all the organisations we had identified we realised that we might actually make a small profit if all the copies were sold, so we amended the final draft of the letter to say that ten per cent of any profit would be donated to charity. The letters went out and we waited.

At first, nothing. Then the telephone started to ring and the postman started to complain about his extra workload and we knew we were up and running. I now started to spend my days writing rather than researching. But not before we rectified some of our mistakes: we discovered that certain words were politically incorrect, our logo was unpopular, our company name ('The Grey Agency') was considered derogatory (we kept the name but amended the logo) and so forth. Even our proposed donation to charity came under some scrutiny—people were suspicious, perhaps fearing that they would end up being investigated by Esther Ranzen!

Lady Thatcher herself, in a conversation with our mutual publisher Eddie Bell, suggested a change of title: 'I don't think of myself as an *ageing parent...*' she said, and she seems to know how to write a good book. In the end we could think of no way of describing the book, although Lady T's comment decided us on one thing—what better person to ask to write the foreword than her daughter Carol?

When all is said and done I have written a book of our time which, I hope, will become an annual publication and which may help families up and down the country to discuss these vital issues, make otherwise difficult decisions and arrange their futures without any shocks or surprises. At the time of going to press every detail is accurate although, by the time you read these words, one or two things are bound to have changed.

Caring for our parents or relations in old age is not someone else's responsibility. It is ours. If you need some help getting started, take a look at the questionnaire on page 15. If you don't know any of the answers talk to the person concerned, naturally using your own judgement about how and when best to ask the questions with some delicacy. Old age is not an issue to be swept aside and ignored. Some consideration now may help you avoid unpleasant or hasty decisions later.

Finally, I should like to thank everyone who has encouraged and helped me over the past year. Please forgive any errors or omissions you may discover—and do tell me about them or request a free Grey Agency Newsletter by dropping me a line at the address below. I plan to send the newsletter to as many readers as request it whenever there is enough new detail to warrant it. Happy reading!

Belinda Hadden
Autumn 1993

The Grey Agency Ltd
Freepost (SW 8500)
PO Box 3054
London SW6 2YY

THE GREY AGENCY

Using this Handbook

As you can see by a quick glance at the table of Contents, I have broken this handbook down into the various relevant areas of life (housing, health, finances, etc.) you and your relatives might want to refer to for help in planning the future. All important addresses are highlighted throughout. Some appear more than once in this handbook, where a given organisation can help in more than one area. I have repeated the address where necessary rather than refer the reader to another part of the book, in the hopes that this will help to make this handbook very 'user friendly'.

Please note that all information in this book is correct at the time of going to press. Neither the author nor the publishers can be held responsible for any addresses, fees or other data that have changed since this time.

QUESTIONNAIRE

- Have you a parent or relatives who will, one day, look to you for advice and support?
- Whom do they see every day?
- Does a neighbour have your telephone number?
- Do they know where to contact you at all times?
- What happens in an emergency?
- In the event of an accident do you know where their nearest hospital is?
- Do you know how to contact their:
    Doctor?
    Bank manager?
    Accountant?
    Solicitor?
    Neighbour?
    Vicar, rabbi, etc.?
- Have you and they ever considered the relative merits of sheltered accommodation, residential care or a nursing home?
- Do you know the difference?
- Do you know what is available locally and what the charges are?
- Are there any further state benefits for which they may be eligible?
- Is there a simple or more sophisticated 'gadget' that might make their lives easier?
- Is their home safe from accidents and break-ins?
- Are you aware of the extensive range of concessions available for older people?
- Have they made a will?
- Do you know where they keep it?
- Who are the executors?
- What *is* a Power of Attorney?
- What practical things need to be done when someone dies?
- Have you ever discussed the subject of funerals?
- Do you know whether they would prefer to be buried or cremated?

chapter one

WHAT IS OLD?

Britain's Ageing Population

> *The length of our days is three score years and ten*
> Psalms 90.10

WHAT *DOES* OLD MEAN? If the end of working and raising a family defines the entry to old age, this can include people in their late forties! But this is how the Centre for Policy on Ageing has defined the 13 million people in the 'Third Age'—one quarter of Britain's adult population.

Legally, 'old age' is any age after 50, as defined by the Friendly Society Act of 1896. The dictionary tells us that 'old' means 'advanced in years' or 'having lived for a relatively long time'.

But whatever it means, it is true to say that 'You're as young as you feel'—more now than ever before with people living longer, healthier and more active lives. The vast majority of older people are fit and well, with a cheerful approach to the freedom that their retirement affords them.

In the past 100 years longevity has almost doubled and the proportion of older people has trebled. In the 1890s a woman could expect to live to be 46; today she will probably live to be 77. By the year 2031, according to the Government publication *Social Trends*: 'those aged 80 and over are projected to number 3.4 million: over 60 per cent more than in 1990.'

THE AGEING POPULATION—CAUSE FOR CONCERN

One in five people in the UK is now over 60 (11.6 million), an increase of 8 per cent in 10 years, with the sharpest rise in the over-85 group (50 per cent).[*] This trend is expected to continue and the numbers will exert an unsustainable strain on State provision of pensions and healthcare, particularly with people retiring earlier either through redundancy or choice. While many older people will have made provision for their later years, many will not, and the burden of support

---

[*] OPCS, 1993

will fall on an already over-burdened State and those still in employment.

In Britain, the number of pensioners is expected to increase from 10 million now to 14 million in 40 years' time, yet the working population will not increase at all. The demographic developments that have led to an ageing population in Britain are characteristic of all developed nations, with a trend towards lower birth rates and reduced mortality at all ages. Trends throughout Europe are broadly similar although the United Kingdom has, after Germany, the highest proportion of the population aged 60+.

As women have children later and parents live longer, there may well be no respite between periods of care. Often, families have to take responsibility for their parents before their own children leave home—and that can cause serious problems if one partner or both are in employment. 1993 was designated The European Year of Older People and Solidarity Between Generations and, as a result, governments are already urging employers 'to consider providing support for employees with eldercare responsibilities, because it is this group that is liable to experience absenteeism, stress and other difficulties likely to affect perfor-mance'.

With a falling population and a growing number of retired people, it has been suggested that the burden of geriatric illness will be so heavy that all qualified female school-leavers will have to enter the NHS just to keep it going. The young will look after the old for a few years but, as pension funds run dry and our indus-tries close down for lack of young blood, we need to seek solutions *now* before the problems become severe.

The costs of long-term care for elderly people, people with physical or learn-ing disabilities and people with a mental illness have increased despite the policy of transferring people from long-stay hospitals to the community. The costs to the Department of Social Security (DSS) of residential care for those unable to live independently have also escalated at a frightening rate. As John Major said at the G7 summit last year: 'We have to find new ways of delivering health care so that we can continue to treat more and more patients within the spending limits we can afford.'

The implications for society are enormous. State pensions currently cost the nation £34.5 billion a year—44 per cent of the total Social Security budget. Elderly people are the main consumers of health and social services in the UK. They are to be found in every type of care environment: general hospitals, residential care and nursing homes, mental health units, the community, day centres and day hospitals. The State's bill for residential care is expected to soar from £7.5 billion now to £30 billion by the year 2031.

Much must be done to keep people healthy and active in their third age, to develop an effective community care service for dependent people and to plan ahead for the problems of the demographic time-bomb which will affect us all.

SOURCES OF INFORMATION

Age Concern England
Astral House
1268 London Road
London SW16 4ER
Tel: 081–679 8000

Age Concern Scotland
54a Fountainbridge
Edinburgh EH3 9PT
Tel: 031–228 5656

Age Concern Wales
Fourth Floor
1 Cathedral Road
Cardiff CF1 9SD
Tel: 0222 371566

Age Concern Northern Ireland
6 Lower Crescent
Belfast BT7 1NR
Tel: 0232 245729

Age Concern is a registered charity whose governing body includes representatives of over 80 national organisations and six departments of state. There are around 1100 independent local Age Concern groups in England. Age Concern England (ACE) works closely with Age Concerns Scotland, Wales and Northern Ireland and provides services to elderly people, stimulates innovation and research and works in partnership with other relevant statutory voluntary bodies.

Age Concern groups provide a wide range of services, often including day care, visiting services, lunch clubs, over 60s clubs and, in some areas, specialist services for physically and mentally frail elderly people. The Information and Training Departments of ACE provide a direct service of advice and support to professionals and volunteers working with elderly people throughout the country. ACE also gives grants to new projects and organisations and acts as an agent for government programmes such as Employment Training and Opportunities for Volunteers. ACE campaigns on many issues affecting elderly people and aims to inform public opinion through national reports, conferences, publicity, campaigning and the promotion of research.

ACE publications include *Your Rights for Pensioners* and numerous leaflets on health, mobility, death and bereavement, financial and legal matters and safety. For example: *Preparing for Retirement* (£12.95) *Old Age Abuse* (£6.95)

Centre for Policy on Ageing
25–31 Ironmonger Row
London EC1V 3QP
Tel: 071–253 1787

The Centre for Policy on Ageing (CPA) was formed in 1947. It promotes informed debate about issues affecting older age groups, stimulates awareness of the needs of older people and encourages the spread of good practice that will enable everyone to live the last third of life as fully as possible. Although CPA's work is primarily directed towards informing and influencing service providers, the fundamental touchstone of its approach is to discover and advocate what older people themselves want and need.

CPA's publications are aimed at all people who work with older people. These publications include analyses of research, policy and practice, and

examine all aspects of life from the viewpoint of the older citizen. For example:
Growing Old Together (£10.50)
CPA World Directory of Old Age (£33)
Aspects of Ageism (£1)

Office of Population, Censuses and Surveys
St Catherine's House
10 Kingsway
London C2B 6LH
Tel: 071–242 0262
The Office of Population Censuses and Surveys (OPCS) provides a breakdown and continuous analysis of United Kingdom statistics on population and demographics, with a summary of the projections. Results from the 1988 survey are now available. Many publications are available and include:
Death by Cause (£2)
Retirement and Retirement Plans (£16)
1991 Census Definitions (£13.80)
   Future monitors will include:
Persons Aged 60 and Over
Limiting Long-Term Illness
Communal Establishments

The Family Policy Studies Centre
231 Baker Street
London NW1 6XE
Tel: 071–486 8211
Family matters are changing and becoming a major issue, with declining marriage rates, increasing cohabitation, divorce, one-parent families and more dual-worker families. We are seeing an increasing need for families to care for an ageing population that has to be balanced with the demands of paid work. The Family Policy Studies

Centre plays an important role in research, social policy and information about family matters. Numerous publications are available, including:
Families in the Future (£3.50)
Disability and Dependency in Old Age (£7.95)
Community Care and Elderly People (£5.45)

The European Family Policies Studies Centre
231 Baker Street
London NW1 6XE
Tel: 071–486 8211
The EFPSC includes among its objectives the analysis of significant European social and demographic trends, the study of their implications for policy and practice and the examination of policy innovations. In particular it is concerned with understanding the demographic trends and contemporary family patterns and changes that are taking place, and the implications of these for policy and practice.

The Host Consultancy
Labour Market Intelligence Unit
Horsham
W. Sussex RH12 1YS
Tel: 0403 211440
The Host Consultancy researches and produces publications concerning the effect of the increasing age of the labour force combined with the rising number of elderly in the population and its impact on care and employment policy.

Population Concern
231 Tottenham Court Road
London W1P 9AE
Tel: 071–637 9582
Population Concern is the interna-

tional division of the UK Family Planning Association and aims to raise awareness of the size and complexity of world population and the resulting effect on social and economic development. It seeks to establish a balance between world population, natural resources and environment, and to raise funds to provide the knowledge and means of planned parenthood.

Counsel and Care (Advice and Help for Older People)
Twyman House
16 Bonny Street
London NW1 9PG
Tel: 071–485 1550
Counsel and Care (C & C) is a registered charity whose aims and objectives are to make available advice and practical help to older people and their carers, friends and relatives. It provides grants where possible and information on services and benefits, and advises those working with older people and those working to improve conditions. It sets out to promote good standards of care and promotes the positive image of older people generally, and comments on a variety of social policy issues

through its links with ministers, MPs, government departments and local and health authorities. C & C publishes a number of leaflets and reports. The following information sheets are available free to individual enquirers who send a large sae (one copy per person):
History of Counsel and Care
Older People in Britain: Fact and
 Fiction
Help at Home
The Social Fund for Older People
Disability Living Allowance
Dementia

Help the Aged
St James Walk
London EC1R 0BE
Tel: 071–253 0253
Help the Aged aims to meet the needs of the frail, isolated and poor elderly people in the UK and overseas, responding to those needs with effective fundraising and aid programmes. Help the Aged promotes a better awareness and understanding of the elderly and offers advice, information and a wide selection of literature about health, care, safety, mobility and special equipment.

Other organisations which monitor old age, its effects and policy thereon, are:

Foundation for Age Research/Research into Ageing
49 Queen Victoria Street
London EC4 4SA
Tel: 071–236 4365

The Policy Studies Institute
100 Park Village East
London NW1 3SR
Tel: 071–387 2171

RETIREMENT COUNSELLING AND COURSES

A number of companies run retirement courses which cover a variety of subjects to prepare people for their retirement. Subjects covered in these courses may include financial planning, savings and investments, legal matters, wills, health, diet, and leisure activities, accommodation alternatives and home improvement.

Further information may be obtained from:

**Pre-Retirement Association of
Great Britain and Northern Ireland**
Nodus Centre
University Campus
Guildford
Surrey GU2 5RX
Tel: 0483 39323

**The Retirement Association of
Northern Ireland**
Room 11
Bryson House
28 Bedford Street
Belfast BT2 7FE
Tel: 0232 321324

Godwins Ltd
Kingsmead
Farnborough
Hants GUl4 7TE
Tel: 0252 521701

**The Retirement Counselling
Service**
Turret House
The Avenue
Bucks HP7 OAB
Tel: 0494 433553

**The British Pensioner and Trade
Union Association**
Norman Dodds House
315 Bexley Road
Erith
Kent DA8 3EZ
Tel: 0322 335464
The Association aims to bring about
improvements in the provisions made
for older people.

Wales Pensioners
Transport House
1 Cathedral Road
Cardiff CF1 9SD
Tel: 0222 225141
Wales Pensioners provides informa-
tion and support for all pensioners
throughout Wales.

Further Reading
An Ageing Population (Family Policy Studies Centre, 1991), £2.50
   General Household Survey 1988, Office of Population, Censuses and Surveys,
Social Survey Division (HMSO, 1990), £16.50

chapter two

HEALTHY LIVING

*All You Need to Know to
Help Your Parents Stay Well*

IT SOMETIMES SEEMS IMPOSSIBLE to keep up with the latest information about what is good and bad for us. One minute 'the authorities' say jogging is the best thing one can do, the next minute it is held responsible for all sorts of long-term problems.

The most important thing to remember is that it is never too late to change one's lifestyle and habits in order to lead a healthier and happier life. Whatever changes are made towards a more balanced diet and regular, gentle exercise will produce benefits which far outweigh any sacrifices.

Fortunately, there is a wealth of literature and advice on hand to advise the best way to stay healthy and get the best out of life. *'Mens sana in corpora sana'*—a healthy mind in a healthy body—still holds good and there is no substitute for keeping fit and mentally alert, eating a healthy, balanced diet and having regular eye and dental check-ups.

Changes happen to everyone as they grow older: hair loses colour, names slip the mind, staircases seem steeper, but there is much you can do to improve the quality of your ageing parent's life and maintain his or her good health into old age. Do not dismiss physical or mental problems as 'just old age'. Many conditions can be treated very easily and successfully; there are a large number of professional people who may be able to help, and there is much that can be done for older people to help themselves.

In recent years there have been many improvements in the quality and range of care available from the NHS, most of which are of particular importance to older people. For example, doctors must now offer an annual health check to all patients aged over 75. And there are a wide range of special clinics, occupational therapists, physiotherapists and specialists to help—all surgeries must now provide a leaflet explaining the range of services available.

Local pharmacists can also advise on health problems, including when to see a doctor. Men over 65 and women over 60 years of age are currently entitled to free prescriptions and they may be able to get help with the cost of dental care, sight tests and glasses. The local authority Social Services Department will advise you as to which services are available. Their address and telephone number can be obtained from the library, Community Health Council, Citizens Advice Bureau or the telephone directory.

NHS PRESCRIPTIONS

Men over 65 and women over 60 are entitled to free prescriptions; those on Income Support or Family Credit are also eligible. In addition, sufferers of various medical conditions and people on War or MOD Disablement Pensions are also eligible; people may also have a low-income entitlement. Leaflet P11 from the Department of Health explains who is eligible and how to claim an exemption certificate. Other Department of Health leaflets are:

AB11—*Help with NHS Costs*
S11—*NHS Dental Treatment*
G11—*NHS Sight Tests and Vouchers for Glasses*
H11—*NHS Hospital Travel Costs*
WF11—*NHS Wigs and Fabric Supports*
P11—*NHS Prescriptions*

These are also available from doctors. AB11 is available from some post offices. All are available from:

The Health Publications Unit
No 2 Site
Heywood Stores
Manchester Road
Heywood
Lancs L10 2PZ

THE HEALTH EDUCATION AUTHORITY

The HEA publishes numerous books and leaflets about all aspects of healthy living which are available free of charge. In addition to numerous other publications about every aspect of health—heart disease, cancer, family health, alcohol, health and hygiene—of particular interest for older people are:

Coping with Change—Focus on Retirement
Resource Materials for Mid-life and Pre-Retirement Programmes
Exercise, Why Bother?
Enjoy Healthy Eating
Enjoy Fruit and Veg—Eat Well, Feel Well, Be Well
Changing What You Eat Pack
Diet and Cancer
Diet, Nutrition and Healthy Eating
Smoking Factpack
Cut Down On Your Drinking

For a booklet detailing all the publications, get in touch with the local health education unit. To find the local health education unit, contact:

Health Education Authority (England)
Hamilton House
Mabledon Place
London WC1H 9TX
Tel: 071–383 3833

Health Education Board for Scotland
Woodburn House
Canaan Lane
Edinburgh EH10 4SG
Tel: 031–447 8044

Health Education Authority for Wales
Brunel House (Eighth Floor)
2 Fitzalan Road
Cardiff DF2 1EB
Tel: 0222 752222

Health Promotion Agency for Northern Ireland
18 Ormeau Avenue
Belfast BT2 8HS
Tel: 0232 311611

Other organisations which produce valuable information and publications:

The British Geriatrics Society
1 St Andrews Place
London NW1 4LB
Tel: 071–935 4004
The Society's goal is the relief of suffering and distress among the aged and infirm. It strives to reach this goal by working towards improving the standards of medical care, holding meetings and encouraging research on special problems. It publishes numerous invaluable leaflets which are available (free if you send a 9-inch x 6-inch sae), including:
How to Look After Your Food...and Yourself
How to Protect Yourself from Influenza
How to Get the Sleep You Need
How to Eat Well When You Are Ill
How to Help Yourself to a Well-Nourished Retirement
How to Keep Warm and Prevent Hypothermia

Help the Aged
St James Walk
London EC1R 0BE
Tel: 071–253 0253
Help the Aged publishes a number of useful advice leaflets which are available free by calling the Seniorline on 0800 289 404, including:
Better Hearing
Better Sight
Eating in Later Life
Fight the Flu
Fitter Feet
Gardening
Keeping Mobile
Managing Your Medicines
Winter Hypothermia

The British Heart Foundation
14 Fitzhardinge Street
London W1H 4DH
Tel: 071–935 0185
Heart disease accounts for nearly half of all deaths in the UK. 'Don't smoke, watch your weight, take regular exercise and choose food wisely' is the

advice from The British Heart Foundation, the largest heart charity. It raises money to fund research into all forms of heart and circulatory disease, education programmes for the public and health professionals, rehabilitation and support groups for heart patients and cardiac equipment for hospitals and ambulance services. It also promotes life-saving training techniques. Many publications are available from the BHF free of charge (donations are welcome) such as the free booklet of recipes *Food Should Be Fun*. A £5 donation is usually asked towards the cost of videos.

The Coronary Prevention Group
102 Gloucester Place
London W1H 3DA
Tel: 071–935 2889

Chest Heart and Stroke Association
Fourth Floor
Tavistock House
Tavistock Square
London WC1H 9JE
Tel: 071–387 3012
A charity specialising is prevention and assistance

SMOKING

It is a myth that smoking doesn't matter if you have smoked all your life without apparent ill effects. It is never too late to feel the benefits of stopping, in fact giving up smoking is the single most effective action anyone can take to improve his or her health.

All forms of smoking are bad: cigarettes, cigars and pipes all increase the risk of heart disease, lung disease (especially bronchitis and lung cancer) and osteoporosis (thinning of the bones). Smoking also reduces the chances of survival after a heart attack.

Many people successfully give up smoking every year and there is plenty of help available. Doctors are only too happy to help and nicotine patches may be available on prescription to help a person quit. In addition, useful leaflets can be obtained from:

Action on Smoking and Health (ASH)
109 Gloucester Place
London
W1H 3PH
Tel: 071–935 3519
For information about smoking and the risks, and campaigning and government policy

QUIT
102 Gloucester Place
London W1H 3DA
Tel: 071–487 2858
QUIT is there to assist those who wish to give up. Their QUITLINE (071–487 3000) offers free, one-to-one advice and referral to local stop smoking groups. Also phone this number for a free QUITPACK.

DIET

It is the food we eat that gives us the energy and nourishment to keep us alive in mind, body and spirit. If diets aren't varied or if a person doesn't eat enough, he or she is more liable to illness. On the other hand, eating too much can also cause health problems.

As metabolic rate slows down it is harder to keep the weight off, and therefore it is important not to snack on the wrong sorts of food: those with a lot of salt or sugar. Similarly, as one gets older, sense of taste may diminish and it is important not to compensate by adding lots of salt. The addition of herbs and spices is a good way to stimulate the appetite.

The most important thing is a well-balanced diet which includes plenty of fruit and vegetables, foods high in starches (carbohydrate) and fibre or roughage where possible (wholemeal bread or potatoes with their skins on if possible), and fish, especially oily fish like mackerel, sardines, tuna or pink salmon. Where possible lean cuts of meat and poultry should be used. The saturated fats found in butter and cream should be taken in moderation. It is important to remember that the body burns more energy in the winter and, therefore, people need to eat more to stay warm.

The British Nutrition Foundation
High Holborn House
52–54 High Holborn
London WC1V 6RQ
Tel: 071–404 6504
The British Nutrition Foundation is an impartial, scientific organisation which sets out to provide reliable information and scientifically based advice on nutrition and related health matters, with the ultimate objective of helping individuals to understand how they may best match their diet with their lifestyle. Its principle functions fall under the headings of information, education and research. The Foundation produces a wide range of publica-tions to suit different levels. In addition, nutrition scientists at the Foundation are happy to answer enquiries by letter or telephone. The BNF is a non-profit-making organisation. Publications include (and are free unless otherwise indicated):
Nutrition and the Elderly
Nutritional Aspects of Fish
Vegetarian Diets
Dietary Influences in Cancer
The Role of Diet in Dental Health
BNF: Nutrition Facts (A5 leaflets, £3.50 per set)
BNF Briefing Papers (A4 booklets, £2.50 each)

The Health Education Authority (see page 27) publishes a free leaflet called *Enjoy Healthy Eating*.

Complan
Crookes Healthcare Ltd
PO Box 57
Central Park
Lenton Lane
Nottingham NG7 2LJ
Tel: 0602 507431
Appetising and nutritious, *Complan* is ideal for convalescents, those unable to face food or those who need an energy-boosting supplement. Available in six flavours, each nutritionally-balanced serving provides 250 calories and a 25 per cent of the recommended daily amount (RDA) of vitamins and minerals. Easy to make with water, *Complan* is available from chemists and supermarkets and contains no artificial colour or preservatives. Write for a *Complan* Carers information pack, or an audio-cassette newsletter which is free to those looking after frail or disabled people at home.

WeightWatchers UK Ltd
Kidwells Park House
Kidwells Park Drive
Maidenhead
Berks S16 8YT
Tel: 0628 777077
If the aim is to lose weight it is important to do it sensibly and not sacrifice a balanced diet and essential vitamins, minerals and nutrients. Sound advice and practice and the address of local WeightWatchers branches are available from WeightWatchers UK Ltd (address above).

The Vegetarian Society of The United Kingdom
Parkdale
Dunham Road
Altrincham
Cheshire, WA14 4QG
Tel: 061–928 0793
The Vegetarian Society's aim is to increase the number of vegetarians in the UK in order to save animals, benefit human health and protect the environment and world food resources. It is a registered charity dedicated to campaigning, information, education and research.

Its leaflet *Healthy Nutrition in Later Life* gives sensible guidelines for a vegetarian diet and all the vital vitamins, minerals and nutrients, energy, fibre and protein requirements. Other factsheets are also available.

The Vegan Society
7 Battle Road
St Leonard's-on-Sea
East Sussex
TN37 7AA
Tel: 0424 427393
Advice and information for a healthy vegan diet

ALCOHOL

In moderation, alcohol is unlikely to cause harm. In fact, a glass of wine a day has been said to reduce stress and lower blood-pressure. But too much can seriously damage health and, in the long term, can lead to stomach disorders, high blood-pressure and brain damage.

Alcohol is more likely to stay in the body for longer in older people. Similarly, they may find that they are affected by a very small amount of alcohol.

Alcohol Concern
275 Gray's Inn Road
London WC1X 8QF
Tel: 071–833 3471

Alcoholics Anonymous
PO Box 1
Stonebow House
Stonebow
York YO1 2NJ
Tel: 0904 644026

Alcohol Problem Advisory Service
4 Greenland Road
London NW1 0AS
Tel: 071–482 1173

Alcohol Counselling and Prevention Services
34 Electric Lane
London SW9
Tel: 071–737 3579

Al-Anon (for Relatives)
61 Great Dover Street
London SE1 4YF
Tel: 071–403 0888
Al-Anon provides understanding and support for the relatives and friends of problem drinkers, whether the alcoholic is still drinking or not. Literature and advice are available.

Age Concern England produces a leaflet: *Safer Drinking for the Over 60s* (for address see page 000).

The Health Education Authority publishes a booklet *That's The Limit: A Guide to Sensible Drinking* (address page 27).

SEXUALITY

Older people can enjoy sex just as much as younger people; indeed, some changes to an older person's body may enhance his or her own (or his or her partner's pleasure). But other changes can cause difficulties. After the menopause women may experience physical changes, for example, vaginal dryness, for which there are a variety of creams and lubricants. Some older men suffer from impotence, through an illness or certain medication that they are taking. Older people should not be embarrassed to seek the help of their doctor for this or any other sexual difficulty.

SPOD
286 Camden Road
London N7 0BJ
Tel: 071–607 8851
SPOD provides information relating to sexuality and the needs of people with a disability. It can provide a wide range of information, advisory leaflets and publications (some free, others between 25p and 50p). Phone for publications list.

KEEPING MENTALLY ACTIVE

Keeping mentally alert is just as important as keeping physically active. For the older person, starting further education, joining a club or course or spending time on a favourite hobby can be both stimulating and rewarding.

The local College of Further Education, Institute of Adult Education or Community College will have a list of the various courses on offer, both in the evening and the daytime. See Chapter 11, 'Hobbies and Interests', for relevant names and addresses.

Many voluntary bodies welcome older people who would like to use their skills to help others and become a valuable help in the community. See Chapter 3, page 58 and Chapter 11, page 174 for further information.

KEEPING WARM IN WINTER

This is a vital part of keeping well. At home, hot meals and hot drinks will keep the body warm, as will a warm bedroom and a hot drink before bed.

The best way to keep warm when going out is to wear several layers of clothing for better insulation. Above all, make sure that the head, hands and feet are well covered, especially if there is to be a long wait in the cold for a bus or train.

- For more information phone the Winter Warmth Line free on 0800 289404 (England and Wales), 0800 838587 (Scotland), 0800 616757 (Northern Ireland).
- Age Concern's factsheet *Help with Heating* gives details of loans, grants, government benefits and other services.
- The British Geriatrics Society leaflet *How to Keep Warm and Prevent Hypothermia* gives valuable advice and information about helping the elderly staying warm and well.
- Seniorline (Freephone 0800 289404) is run by Help the Aged and British Gas for free information and advice.
- Help the Aged publishes two leaflets: *Winter* and *Hypothermia*. Details can be found in Chapter 3 (page 49).
- Also see Chapter 6 (page 112) on the Social Fund, special payments in cold weather.

The following energy agencies may be able to offer help and information on energy waste, insulation and conservation, safety, payment and pre-payment terms and budget accounts:

Domestic Coal Consumers Council
Freepost
London SW1P 2YZ
Tel: 071–233 0583

Energy Action Grants Agency
Bank Chambers
9–17 Collingwood Street
Newcastle upon Tyne NE1 1JL
Tel: 0800 181 667

Neighbourhood Energy Action
2–4 Bigg Market
Newcastle upon Tyne NE1 1UW
Tel: 091–261 5677

Office of Electricity Regulation (OFFER)
Hagley House
Hagley Road
Edgbaston
Birmingham B16 8QG
Tel: 021–456 6208
OFFER can supply the names of the regional electricity companies, all of whom publish a code of practice leaflet for elderly and disabled people on how to conserve energy, and detailing special switches and controls and the addresses of companies who can supply this equipment.

The Office of Gas Supply
Southside
105 Victoria Street
London
SW1E 6QT
Tel: 071–828 0898

Further Reading
Dangerous Cold: Hypothermia and Cold-related Illness in Older People, Evan Lloyd (Age Concern Scotland (address page 48), 1987), £1.50

EYES

It is normal for people's eyesight to change as they get older. For example, they may find that they have to hold books at arm's length to read them.

It makes sense for older people to have regular sight tests to check the health of their eyes and see whether they need glasses, or whether their glasses need changing. These tests are done by an optometrist or ophthalmic optician. They may be entitled to a free NHS sight test and an NHS Spectacle Voucher if they are on a low income. They can apply for this on form AG1, obtainable from their optician, doctor or local Social Security office.

Two common eye conditions that affect older people are both treatable. Cataracts can be treated through a straightforward operation. Glaucoma can be treated with eye drops, tablets or surgery. People with glaucoma and their close relatives aged 40+ are entitled to free sight tests.

To help your ageing parent's eyes, make sure that there is good lighting in his or her home, particularly for activities like reading and sewing. By placing lights near to where they are needed, one can avoid having to use a stronger bulb. A bright light over the stairs and in other places where people might trip is very important, especially if they have to get up in the night.

Further information is available from:

The Optical Information Council
57a Old Woking Road
W. Byfleet
Surrey KT14 6LF
Tel 0932 353238
Leaflets free with sae

The Eye Care Information Bureau
PO Box 294
London SE1 8NE
Tel: 071–928 9435

Royal National Institute for the Blind
224 Great Portland Street
London W1N 6AA
Tel: 071–388 1266
The RNIB publishes a selection leaflets on eye conditions, prevention and treatment.

Partially Sighted Society
Redbridge House
7 Manor Road
Woodford Bridge
Essex IG8 8ER
Tel: 081 559 2779

The International Glaucoma Association
Kings College Hospital
Denmark Hill
London SE5 9RS
Tel: 071–242 6222
Promotes prevention by means of research and public awareness. Information booklets are available free with sae.

HEARING

There are 7.5 million people in Great Britain with some degree of hearing loss. As they grow older, many people lose the ability to hear high-pitched sounds. If someone you know finds it hard to follow a conversation or hear the telephone or the television, contact a GP. There may be a simple cause such as wax in the ears which can be easily removed (don't try to do it yourself and *never* poke anything in the ears).

Hearing aids are free through the NHS to everyone who needs them, as are batteries and repairs. It takes time to get used to them but do advise your parent to be patient and, if he or she has problems or the hearing aid stops working properly, do take it back.

If someone you know has difficulty hearing the telephone, doorbell or television, they can get special equipment. They should ask their local Social Services Department or see Chapter 8, page 153 of this book.

The Royal National Institute for Deaf People
105 Gower Street
London WC1E 6AM
Tel: 071–387 8033
Text: 071–388 6038
Qwerty 300 band
Minicom 071–383 3154

THE ROYAL NATIONAL INSTITUTE FOR DEAF PEOPLE

The RNID is the UK's largest voluntary organisation representing the needs of deaf, deafened, hard of hearing and deaf-blind people. The RNID provides a range of quality services, including deaf awareness training, assistive devices (through Sound Advantage), information, specialist telephone services (through Typetalk), communication support and residential care for deaf people with special needs. The RNID also raises awareness about the needs of deaf people and campaigns

to remove discrimination and create full access to information. Publications (free) include:
RNID Services and Information
Deaf and Hard of Hearing People
The Ear and How it Works
Let Your Fingers do the Talking
Questions about Tinnitus
Hearing Aids, Questions and Answers

Hearing Concern—The British Association of the Hard of Hearing
7–11 Armstrong Road
London W3 7JL
Tel: 081–743 1110 (voice and minicom)
The Association provides advice, information and support for anyone with acquired hearing loss. It provides information on hearing aids, lip-reading and equipment to help with the television, telephone, etc. It also operates the sympathetic hearing scheme, to raise public awareness of the communication needs of hard of hearing people, and produces a quarterly magazine, *Hearing Concern*. Most publications are free with sae, including:
Facing Up to Hearing Loss
Lip-Reading
How Clearly Do You Speak?
You and Your Hearing Aid

Breakthrough Deaf-Hearing Integration
Charles Gillett Centre
998 Bristol Road
Selly Oak
Birmingham B29 6LE
Tel: 021–472 6447
Text: 021–471 1001
A voluntary organisation that integrates deaf and hearing people of all ages through self-help programmes of social activities, practical projects and training. These show that, through improved communication, deaf people can achieve even greater independence and share, with hearing people, a better quality of life.

Facilities at the Birmingham Centre include a Total Communication Course and an open learning centre, self-help contact groups for all ages, a youth group and an information and library service.

The British Deaf Association
38 Victoria Place
Carlisle CA1 1HU
Tel: 0228 48844
The Association gives information, advice and support for the profoundly deaf and campaigns on behalf of deaf people who use sign language. It produces a wide range of publications, magazines and videos and arranges holidays for older deaf people, conferences and health promotion and has the largest membership organisation in the UK led by deaf people.

Local branches throughout the country arrange group activities, holidays and education and supply publications—list on request.

British Tinnitus Association
Room 6
14–18 West Bar Green
Sheffield S1 2DA
Tel: 0742 796600
This charity gives information, leaflets and advice for tinnitus sufferers. In addition, the Tinnitus helpline is available on Tel: 0354 090210, Monday to Friday 10 a.m. to 3 p.m.

**National Association Of Deaf
People**
103 Heath Road
Widnes
Cheshire WA8 7NU
Tel: 0494 482355

The National Deaf-Blind League
18 Rainbow Court
Paston Ridings
Peterborough PE4 6UP
Tel: 0733 573511

Further Reading
Living with Tinnitus, Richard Hallam (Thorsons, 1993), £5.99.

TEETH

With proper care a person should be able to keep his or her teeth for a lifetime. Brushing well every day with fluoride toothpaste and avoiding eating sugary foods certainly helps.

It is as important to take as much care of false teeth as of natural teeth. They should be cleaned carefully and the wearer should visit the dentist regularly. Whether the teeth are real or false, a dentist should examine the elderly person's mouth from time to time; he or she may be able to make a house call if the patient is housebound.

People on a low income may get help with the cost of dental treatment. Leaflet D11 explains how to get help and is obtainable from dentists or local Social Security offices.

Age Concern England publishes a free factsheet: *Dental Care in Retirement* (see page 48 for address).

BONES

Many older people suffer from osteoporosis, a condition where the bones become thinner and weaker and more susceptible to breaking. This can be prevented or treated. The National Osteoporosis Society runs national education campaigns to work towards eradicating this preventable bone disease. The Society aims to increase awareness and to provide advice on prevention and treatment, information and support for sufferers through patient literature, a national helpline and a network of local groups. This is the only charity raising funds for research into the causes, treatment and prevention of osteoporosis and working nationally and locally to ensure that sufferers can obtain the treatment and support they need. Send sae for further information to:

The National Osteoporosis Society
PO Box 10
Radstock
Bath BA3 3YB
Tel: 0761 432472

FEET

Looking after one's feet is vital whatever one's age, as minor problems can easily lead to major ones. Older people should make sure that shoes fit well and are comfortable, and should try not to wear slippers all day. Chiropodists can provide very useful assistance, from help in cutting toenails to treatment for corns and bunions. If anyone you care for has a problem finding shoes that will fit, contact a specialist footwear company (see Chapter 8, page 155). A GP will be able to put him or her in touch with an NHS chiropodist.

The Society of Chiropodists
53 Welbeck Street
London W1M 7HE
Tel: 071–486 3381
Can offer books, leaflets, and details of local chiropodists

British Footwear Manufacturers Association
Royalty House
72 Dean Street
London W1V 5HB
Tel: 071–437 5573
For advice on specialist footwear manufacturers

GIDDINESS

This is common with older people and can often be treated. Doctors provide useful help and advice. It is important for the affected person not to get up or turn suddenly and, if an older person does feel giddy, he or she should try to sit or lie down for a few minutes, or hold on to something secure until he or she feels steady again.

MEDICINES

To use medicines safely, do observe the following precautions:

- Make sure that whoever is taking them takes them exactly as prescribed or according to the instructions.
- No one should ever take them after the expiry date.
- Never mix prescribed and bought medicines without first checking with the doctor or pharmacist who prescribed them.
- Dispose safely of any medicines no longer in use.
- Keep all medicines out of reach of children.
- Consult a doctor about whether alcohol will react badly with any medicines being taken.

Further information on safety with medicines is in Chapter 9.

INCONTINENCE

Urinary and faecal incontinence are distressing for sufferers—many are afraid of leaving the house lest they should have an accident. A great deal of help is available so that even severe cases can be managed with the help of special garments, pads, appliances and deodorants. Doctors or District Nurses should be able to prescribe these aids.

The Continence Foundation
2 Doughty Street
London WC1N 2PH
Tel: 071–404 6875
The Continence Foundation operates a confidential information helpline staffed by experienced nurse continence advisers who can answer queries about all aspects of bladder and bowel problems. The helpline operates Monday to Friday, 2 p.m. to 7 p.m. on 091–213 0050. Letters can also be answered (please include sae). A range of information leaflets and a mail order book service are also available.

Association of Continence Advisers
380 Harrow Road
London W9 2HU
Tel: 071–289 6111
The Association can supply leaflets and information for local advice groups.

Disabled Living Foundation
380–384 Harrow Road
London W9 2HU
Tel: 071–289 6111
The Disabled Living Foundation offers an advisory service and a number of publications about incontinence, stress incontinence, adult bedwetting and bowel problems (priced between £1.50 and £8.50—send sae for publications lists).

Further Reading
Age Concern England has produced a set of ten leaflets about urinary and faecal incontinence. Please send sae (address page 48) for a publications list.

Counsel and Care for the Elderly has produced a leaflet, *A Positive Approach to Incontinence for Older People*, which is available free with sae (address page 49).

Overcome Incontinence, Richard J. Millard (Thorsons, 1993), £5.99

The following associations provide information and local self-help groups for anyone living with a urostomy, colostomy or ileostomy:

Colostomy Welfare Group
38 Eccleston Square
London SW1V 1PB
Tel: 071–828 5175

Coronary Prevention Group
102 Gloucester Place
London W1H 3HR
Tel: 071–935 2889

**Ileostomy Association of Great
Britain and Northern Ireland**
Amblehurst House
Black Scotch Lane
Mansfield
Notts NG18 4PF
Tel: 0623 28099

The Urostomy Association
Buckland
Beaumont Park
Danbury
Essex
Tel: 0245 224294

EXERCISE

It is never too late to start and exercise is good for you at any age. However, it is sensible to consult a doctor first if your parent or relative has been ill or is unused to physical activity.

Exercise improves strength, suppleness and stamina. Activities like gardening, bowls, dancing and walking are all excellent forms of exercise. Swimming is particularly good if a person is overweight or has any backache, stiffness or disability, as the water supports the body.

Many local authorities offer older people reduced rates of entry and special classes at sports centres and, if they do not, it may be possible to arrange through the sport and recreation department at the local town hall. Information on local keep fit, exercise or swimming classes may be obtained at the local library or town hall. A number of organisations exist to help people to start their own swimming groups, yoga classes or even windsurfing team—further details of these are given in Chapter 11.

The Dark Horse Venture
Kelton
Woodlands Road
Liverpool L17 0AN
Tel: 051–729 0092
The Dark Horse Venture encourages order people to take up new activities and discover hidden talents, encouraged by someone with professional training or proven experience in your chosen activity. One of the activity categories is 'Exploring and Exercising', which encourages people to undertake travel, explorations or physical recreation. See Chapter 11 for further details.

Yoga for Health Foundation
Ickwell Bury
Biggleswade
Beds SG18 9EF
Tel: 0767 627271
Special courses for 'third age' guests are held during the year, led by lecturers and teachers all of whom are over 70. The courses are aimed at maximising abilities and gaining as much as possible from later years. The Yoga for Health Centre is open all year round and welcomes senior guests at any time, aiming to provide a balanced programme which benefits older people, including those with chronic disability. The Centre is modified for wheelchair use and provides a care staff throughout the day.

Relaxation for Living
168–170 Oatlands Drive
Weybridge
Surrey KT13 9ET
Tel: 0932 858355
Relaxation for Living is a national educational charity founded in 1972. It exists to promote the teaching of physical relaxation to combat the stress, strain, anxiety and tension of modern life and to reduce fatigue. The charity offers a free information pack, a quarterly newsletter (£7 p.a.), audio tapes, leaflets, books, courses in relaxation and stress management, a correspondence course and courses to train teachers in relaxation and stress management.

Thirteen leaflets are available priced from 25p–35p, or you can get a set of leaflets for £3.

The Medau Society
8b Robson House
East Street
Epsom
Surrey KT17 1HH
Tel: 0372 729056
The Medau Society trains teachers in the Medau System of teaching rhythmic movement, which can be adapted to need the needs of all ages and abilities. Medau classes improve posture, co-ordination, muscle tone and suppleness. Active recreational classes and chair-based exercise classes are available when appropriate; free literature and information are available with sae. Telephone for the address of local Medau classes.

Extend Exercise Training Ltd
1a North Street
Sheringham
Norfolk NR26 8LJ
Tel: 0263 822479
Music and movement classes for over-60s and disabled people of all ages.

The Women's League of Health and Beauty
Walter House
418 The Strand
London WC2R OPT
Tel: 071–240 8456
The 280 centres in the UK cater for women of all ages.

FURTHER HELP AND ADVICE ON PREVENTION AND TREATMENT

The Medical Department
The Wellcome Foundation
Crewe Hall
Crewe
Cheshire CW1 1UB
Tel: 0270 583151
The Medical Department provides patients with information leaflets on a variety of conditions such as shingles, genital herpes and HIV.

The Alzheimer's Disease Society (England)
Gordon House
10 Greencoat Place
London SW1P 1PH
Tel: 071–306 0606
Alzheimer's Disease is a physical disease which causes a progressive decline in the ability to remember, to learn, to think and to reason. The Society gives support for families of Alzheimer's Disease sufferers, provides literature and has a national

network of support groups.

The Society offers assistance through membership, branches and support groups to provide practical help, information and guidance for carers and professionals. The society also campaigns for adequate and high-quality services and promotes research and public awareness. A large number of publications are available from the society, on Alzheimer's and other illnesses—phone for a publications list. The free recorded information numbers are:

Alzheimer's Disease: 0800 318771
Other Dementias: 0800 318772
The Society—How We Help:
 0800 318773
Who Can Help—Services:
 0800 318774
Legal and Financial Information:
 0800 318775

Alzheimer's Scotland
8 Hill Street
Edinburgh EH2 3JZ
Tel: 031–225 1453
Helpline: 031–220 6155 (24 hours)
Alzheimer's Scotland exists to help people with dementia and their carers with a network of local groups and branches which provide a chance for carers to meet others in their situation.

Projects around Scotland provide services such as home support and day centres in order to give carers a valuable break and to provide stimulation and social contact for the person with dementia. Many publications are available, priced 10p to £2—send sae for a publications list.

Alzheimer's Disease Society (Wales)
Tonne Hospital
Neath
West Glamorgan SA11 3LX
Tel: 0639 641938

Alzheimer's Disease Society (Northern Ireland)
11 Wellington Park
Belfast BT9 6DJ
Tel: 0232 664400

Dementia Services Development Centre
University of Stirling
Stirling FK9 4LA
Tel: 0786 467740
This is the research centre which exists to extend and improve services to people with dementia and their carers. It provides information, development assistance, conferences and seminars, publications, research and training.

Further Reading
Caring for Confusion, Paulette Micklewood (Scutari Press, 1991) is a book about the care of patients with Alzheimer's Disease.
 See also 'Mental Health', below.

The Arthritis and Rheumatism Council
PO Box 177
Chesterfield
Derbyshire S41 7TQ
Tel: 0246 558033

Only one person in 50 will escape arthritis or rheumatism to one degree or another; in Britain these afflictions affect up to eight million people severely. The Arthritis and Rheumatism Council funds research to find a cure and publishes over 40 free booklets and leaflets to help people understand and cope with their illness.

Arthritis Care
18 Stephenson Way
London NW1 2HD
Tel: 071–916 1500
Helpline: 0800 289170
This is a major voluntary organisation working with and for people of all ages with arthritis and rheumatism. Services include holidays, counselling, mobility equipment, leaflets and information.

The Arthritic Association
Hill House
Little New Street
London EC4A 3TR
Tel: 071–491 0233

Further Reading
Life without Arthritis—The Maori Way, Jan de Vries (Mainstream Publishing, 1991), £4.99

The National Back Pain Association
31–33 Park Road
Teddington
Middlesex TW11 0AB
Tel: 081–977 5474
The only charity devoted entirely to back pain, the NBPA funds research into causes and treatment of back pain and educates people to use their bodies sensibly and reduce the risks of back pain. The Association runs nationwide branches to help sufferers and offers a range of publications, many of which are free:
Self-care
Better Backs for Gardeners
Better Backs for Drivers
Obtaining Treatment from
    Chiropractors, Osteopaths and
    Physiotherapists

Further Reading
Back Pain, Roger Newman Turner (Thorsons, 1993), £5.99

The Chartered Society of Physiotherapy
14 Bedford Row
London WC1R 4ED
Tel: 071–242 1941
The Society helps to promote good health and publishes a range of leaflets and pamphlets which are free with sae. For instance:
Physiotherapy and Older People
Mobility is a Must
Look After Your Back
Take The Strain Out of Gardening

BACUP (The British Association of Cancer United Patients, Their Families and Friends)
3 Bath Place
Rivington Street
London EC2A 3JR
Tel: 071–613 2121 (admin only)
Info: 0800 181199
BACUP offers up-to-date information and emotional support to people with cancer, their families and friends. Free, confidential services include a nationwide telephone information service staffed by cancer nurses.

A London-based one-to-one counselling service is available to patients, families, friends and colleagues who feel that cancer is affecting their lives. Appointments may be made on 071–696 9000.

BACUP publishes over 40 booklets on different cancers and their treatments and on the practical and emotional issues faced by people with cancer. The books are clearly written and a publications list is available with sae.

Cancer Relief Macmillan Fund

Living with cancer

Anchor House
15–19 Britten Street
London SW3 3TY
Tel: 071–351 7811
The fund works to improve the quality of life for people with cancer. It builds and maintains day care and in-patient centres, funds a medical education programme to improve the cancer care skills of NHS nurses and doctors, gives grants directly to patients in need and funds four associate charities which provide information and support.

The charity is perhaps best known for Macmillan nurses: trained specialists in caring for people with cancer. There are now more than 950 Macmillan nurses in the UK, offering advice and support at all stages of the illness and in any setting—home, hospital and care centres. Macmillan nurses work with the NHS at all times.

Cancer Help Centre
Grove House
Cornwallis Grove
Clifton
Bristol BS8 4PG
Tel: 0272 743216

Cancer Help runs a holistic healing programme to complement medical treatment, with a one-day or one-week residential course.

The Hodgkin's Disease Association
PO Box 275
Haddenham
Aylesbury
Bucks HP17 8RU
Tel: 0844 291500
The Association offers emotional and practical support and literature for sufferers of Hodgkin's Disease (cancer of the lymphatic system) and their friends and relatives.

Cancerlink
46 Pentonville Road
London N1 9HF
Tel: 071–833 2451
Cancerlink offers cancer patients, their friends and relatives support, literature and an information service.

Cancer Aftercare
21 Zetland Road
Redland
Bristol BS6 7AH
Tel: 0272 427419
Cancer Aftercare offers self-help groups throughout the UK.

The British Diabetic Association
10 Queen Anne Street
London W1M 0BD
Tel: 071–323 1531
The BDA offers information and education for diabetics, professionals and their families; support of medical and social research, local branches and self-help groups.

Further Reading
Diets to Help Diabetes, Martin Budd (Thorsons, 1994), £2.99

Action for Dysphasic Adults
Canterbury House
Royal Street
London SE1 7LN
Tel: 071–261 9572
Dysphasia is a communication handicap resulting from the loss or impairment of speech and language after a stroke or head injury. This organisation provides information and advice for sufferers and their carers. It supports research and development of new methods of assessment and treatment and aims to increase awareness of the abilities and needs of sufferers.

National Eczema Society
Tavistock House North
Tavistock Square
London WC1H 9SR
Tel: 071–388 4097

The Haemophilia Society
123 Westminster Bridge Road
London SE1 7HR
Tel: 071–928 2020

Depressives Associated
PO Box 5
Castle Town
Portland
Dorset DT5 1BQ
Tel: 081 760 0544

MIND
National Association for Mental Health
22 Harley Street
London W1N 2ED
Tel: 071–637 0741

Richmond Fellowship for Mental Welfare
8 Addison Road
Kensington
London W1N
Tel: 071–603 6373

Scottish Action on Dementia
33 Castle Street
Edinburgh EH3 3DN
Tel: 031–220 4886

Multiple Sclerosis Society
25 Effie Road
London SW6 1EE
Tel: 071–736 6267

The Parkinson's Disease Society of the United Kingdom
22 Upper Woburn Place
London WC1H 0RA
Tel: 071–383 3513
The Parkinson's Disease Society exists to help all people with Parkinson's Disease, their families, friends and the professionals involved in their care. The areas of work include welfare, research, information, education, publicity and fundraising. There are approximately 200 local branches offering self-help and mutual support. The Society can provide many books and leaflets about the disease, some of which are free with sae. Send for a publications list.

The Stroke Association
CHSA House
Whitecross Street
London EC1Y 8JJ
Tel: 071–490 7999
The Stroke Association is the only

national charity solely concerned with combating strokes. It funds research and helps stroke patients and their families through advice, publication and welfare grants. It has 20 regional information centres and its community services, dysphasic support and family support schemes provide (in many areas) home visits for stroke victims and their families to help with speech problems and provide emotional support. More than 400 stroke clubs are affiliated to the Association; details of local groups are available on request.

Volunteer Stroke Scheme
7 Albion Street
London W2 2AS
Tel: 071–262 8385
VSS provides help for people who suffer from speech and other problems as a result of a stroke.

Motor Neurone Disease Association
38 Hazelwood Road
Northampton NN1 1LN
Tel: 0604 22269

ALTERNATIVE MEDICINE

The Institute of Complementary Medicine
4 Tavern Quay
Plough Way
Surrey Quay
London SE16 1QZ
Tel: 071–237 5165

The British Acupuncture Association and Register
179 Gloucester Place
London NW1 6DX
Tel: 071–724 5330

The Register of Traditional Chinese Medicine
19 Trinity Road
London N2 8JJ
Tel: 081–883 8431

The British School of Osteopathy
1–4 Suffolk Street
London SW1Y 4GH
Tel: 071–930 9254
The BSO is building a community care clinic for the treatment of disabled people and provides a low-fee system for the treatment of elderly people.

The British Chiropractic Association
29 Whitley Street
Reading
Berks RG2 0EG
Tel: 0734 757557

The British Homoeopathic Association
27a Devonshire Street
London W1N 1RJ
Tel: 071–935 2163

Society of Homoeopaths
2 Artisan Road
Northampton NN1 4HU
Tel: 0604 21400

The National Institute of Medical Herbalists
9 Palace Gate
Exeter EX1 1JA
Tel: 0392 426022

The Incorporated Society of Registered Naturopaths
328 Harrogate Road
Leeds LS17 6PR
Tel: 0532 685 992

The Register of Qualified Aromatherapists
54a Gloucester Avenue
London NW1 8JD

The National Federation of Spiritual Healers
Old Manor Farm Studio
Church Street
Sunbury on Thames
Middlesex TW16 6RG
Tel: 0932 783164

Further Reading
Better Health through Natural Healing, Ross Trattler (Thorsons, 1993), £7.99
   The Complete System of Chinese Self-healing, Dr Stephen T. Chang (Thorsons, 1994), £6.99
   The Science of Homoeopathy, George Vithoulkas (Thorsons, 1993), £14.99

SPECIALIST HEALTH PRODUCTS

Axiom
Harrington Dock
Liverpool X
L70 1AX
Tel: 051–708 7777
Physiotherapy products such as 'trim step' exercisers

Portopaedic Products
Willowmead
Shutlanehead
Newcastle under Lyme
Staffs ST5 4DS
Back supports

Mondial Ltd
Parkside House
17 East Parade
Harrogate
N. Yorks HG1 5LF
Tel: 0423 527797
Rheumatism bands and other aids

Further Reading
The Book of Pain Relief, Leon Chaitow (Thorsons, 1993), £6.99
   Keeping Well—A Guide to Health in Retirement, Anne Roberts (Faber and Faber, 1991), £4.99
   Look Younger, Feel Better: A Top-to-toe Programme for Health and Vitality, Dr James Scala and Barbara Jacques (Piatkus Books, 1993), £9.95
   The Magic of Movement: A Tonic for Older People, Laura Mitchell (Age Concern, 1988), £3.95
   The New Case for Exercise (Health Education Authority, tel: 071–383 3833), £2.95

Take Care of Yourself (Help the Aged, 1988), £2.50. Write to Allyson Mountford, Help the Aged, St James Walk, London WC1R 1BE

You Can Feel Good Again, Richard Carlson (Thorsons, 1993), £4.99

Your Health in Retirement—An A to Z Guide, J.A. Muir (Age Concern, 1990), £4.50

WHO CARES?

Organisations to Turn to for Assistance, Counselling,
Friendship and Practical Advice

OVER THE CENTURIES a massive network of caring organisations has emerged to assist and advise people from all walks of life with all manner of problems.

With so many caring organisations that exist to provide advice, counselling, financial grants or accommodation, it is sometimes hard to know which does what or, indeed, that they exist at all.

I have listed many of the charities that are concerned with health and diseases in Chapter 2, as most are concerned with prevention as well as care and assistance.

Age Concern England
Astral House
1268 London Road
London SW16 4ER
Tel: 081–679 8000

Age Concern Northern Ireland
6 Lower Crescent
Belfast BT17 1NR
Tel: 0232 245729

Age Concern Scotland
54a Fountainbridge
Edinburgh EH3 9PT
Tel: 031–228 5656

Age Concern in Wales
Fourth Floor
1 Cathedral Road
Cardiff CF1 9SD
Tel: 0222 371566

Age Concern England (ACE) is the main charity concerned with research, aid, training and publications for older people. Together with its affiliated organisations Age Concern Scotland, Ireland and Wales, ACE provides a wide range of community services, including day centres, lunch clubs, visits for the lonely as well as transport and many other schemes. It also takes an active part in policy formulation by advising the UK Government on legislation affecting older people and campaigning on their behalf. ACE publishes information sheets on the following subjects (send sae for a maximum of five): health, heating, holidays, wills, bereavement, legal matters, accommodation, finance, education, and disability.

Age Concerns throughout Britain

also exist to promote effective care of and to encourage choice and opportunity for older people. Relevant publications include:

Finding Help at Home
Abuse of Elderly People, Guidelines for Action (25p)

Help the Aged
St James's Walk
London EC1R 0BE
Tel: 071–253 0253

Help the Aged works to improve the quality of life of elderly people, particularly those who are frail, isolated or poor. The charity is primarily a fundraising organisation, making grants to community-based projects.

Help the Aged's Seniorline is a free national information service staffed by advice workers who can respond to callers' questions about housing, health, welfare and disability benefits, mobility, support for carers, community alarms, sources of local practical help and other voluntary organisations. If they are unable to help they can usually tell you who can. Call free on 0800 289404, Monday to Friday, 10 a.m. to 4 p.m.

The charity also has a range of free advice leaflets on welfare and disability benefits, money matters, home safety and health. Help the Aged also cares for nearly 600 residents in its nine extra-sheltered developments, 32 semi-sheltered dwellings, four registered residential homes and many donated properties. Free leaflets cover health, disability, finance, safety and security, health, bereavement, housing, law, equipment, loneliness and hypothermia. Send sae for a publications list (also see the relevant chapters of this book).

Counsel and Care for The Elderly
Twyman House
16 Bonny Street
London NW1 9PG
Tel: 071–485 1550

Counsel and Care offers free, confidential advice, practical help and an information service for older people, their carers and families and health professionals. It can supply grants to support older people in residential or nursing homes, or in their own homes and, where possible, can access financial resources administered by other agencies for the benefit of older people and their carers. It updates information on services and benefits for older people by visiting residential and nursing establishments, building up and revising details of the resources available. If Counsel and Care cannot help callers it is usually able to direct them to whoever can.

A wide range of information sheets, reports and leaflets are available—these include: *Community Care Services for Older People*, *Which Charity*, *Help at Home* and *Community Care Services for Older People*. Send sae for a publications list.

CARERS

If you are caring for a relative or friend who has an illness or disability that makes daily life difficult, you could claim money and receive other kinds of support. A leaflet, *Caring for Someone?* produced by the DSS, details:

- the help available from Social Security and your local council, including information on benefits and allowances, and protecting state pension rights (see Chapter 6, page 98)
- information on practical help such as District Nurses and home helps or someone to give you a break from caring
- a list of useful telephone numbers and addresses.

The Citizens Advice Bureau can advise on problems relating to help and care at home and, if they cannot help you themselves, invariably know who can. See page 97 for national headquarters or look in the phone book or in the Yellow Pages under 'Social Service and Welfare Organisations'.

The Health Education Authority publishes:

Who Cares? Information and support for Carers of Confused People (30p)
Working With Carers (£3.95)
Call for Care (£1.95)

A booklet is available detailing other title and prices is available from them at:
Hamilton House
Mabledon Place
London WC1H 9TX
Tel: 071–383 3833

The Carers National Association (England)
29 Chilworth Mews
London W2 3RG
Tel: 071–490 8818

CNA Scotland
11 Queen's Crescent
Glasgow G4 9AS
Tel: 041–333 9495
This voluntary organisation gives valuable information and support to people who are caring at home, as well as advice and information through their wide range of free leaflets. There are branches and local offices throughout the UK—for local details contact either office above.

The Princess Royal Trust for Carers
16 Byward Street
London EC3R 5BA
Tel: 071–480 7788
The Trust aims to raise funds in order to enter into funding partnership to set up carer centres in each local authority area.

The Association of Crossroads Care Attendant Schemes (England)
10 Regent Place
Rugby
Warwickshire CV21 2PN
Tel: 0788 573653

ACCAS Wales
5 Cooper's Yard
Curran Road
Cardiff CF1 5DF
Tel: 0222 222282

ACCAS Scotland
24 George Square
Glasgow G2 1EG
Tel: 041–226 3793
This Association provides care attendants who come into the home to give the carers of disabled people a break.

There are 180 autonomous schemes and eight regional offices throughout England, Scotland and Wales.

SEMI Care Trust
Kingsley House
Greenbank Road
Bristol BS5 6HE
Tel: 0272 525325
SEMI Care is a voluntary agency which provides trained sitters, day care and counselling to Alzheimer's Disease or dementia patients or their carers in Bristol and the surrounding area. The hourly rate for sitters is £2.

The National Extension College
18 Brooklands Avenue
Cambridge CB2 2HN
Tel: 0223 316644

The National Extension College is an education charity providing long-distance learning course for adult learners and resource materials for use in a wide range of educational and training areas. Their Caring and Health materials can provide guidance, support and skills for all carers, whether they are looking after someone at home, working in the community or within the Health Service. Titles include:
Caring at Home—Information and Advice Aiming to Combat Isolation and Helplessness (£6.95)
Coming into Hospital—An Information Booklet for Patients (£15)
Coping with the System—An Outline Guide to the Citizen's Everyday Rights (£15.95)

The Winged Fellowship (see page 86 for details) offers a series of special weeks of holidays for Alzheimer's Disease sufferers and their carers each year.

If someone needs practical services at home, the Social Services Department of the local council should be able to assist, depending on where he or she lives. These services may include the following:

- home care help
- chiropody at home
- laundry or incontinence service
- hairdressing at home
- gardening, decorating, minor repairs
- transport to the shops or to clubs and day centres
- leisure activities for housebound people
- equipment loans
- mobile library services
- visiting schemes
- meals on wheels.

Meals on Wheels provides hot, midday meals for people who cannot prepare their own food, often assisted by the Women's Royal Voluntary Service and the British Red Cross Society with transport. There is a small charge for this service.

The Social Services Department is also responsible for social workers and home care help, and for assessing care needs for either care in the home or referral to a residential or nursing home. The appropriate department can be contacted either by looking under 'Social Services' in the local telephone directory or through the Citizens Advice Bureau (see below).

The National Association of Citizens Advice Bureaux (NACAB)
115–123 Pentonville Road
London N1 9LZ
Tel: 071–833 2181
There are over 1000 Citizens Advice Bureaux in the UK providing information and advice free of charge on every subject. These include financial and legal matters, and consumer and employment problems. To find your nearest CAB phone the NACAB office or look in your telephone directory.

Someone to Talk to

Age Concern has produced a number of publications about caring and carers. *Information for Carers* gives advice on how to cope and whom to contact should you reach crisis point.

The British Association for Counselling
1 Regent Place
Rugby
Warwicks CV21 2PJ
Tel: 0788 578328

Counselling Information Scotland
Scottish Health Education Group
Woodburn House
Canaan Lane
Edinburgh EH10 4SG
Tel: 031–452 8989
BAC and CIS provide lists of counsellors divided into counties, giving the counsellor's qualifications, type of problems counselled and probable cost, and an information sheet about counselling guidelines.

The Samaritans (National Headquarters)
10 The Grove
Slough S4 1QP
Tel: 0753 532713
Samaritans is a voluntary organisation offering confidential emotional support 24 hours a day. There are 171 branches in England, Scotland and Wales—for your nearest branch look in your telephone directory.

Relate/National Marriage Guidance
Herbert Gray College
Little Church Street
Rugby
Warwicks CV21 3AP
Tel: 0788 573241/560811
Local organisations throughout the UK offering relationship counselling. Write to locate your local branch or see your telephone directory.

The National Association of Widows
54–57 Allison Street
Digbeth
Birmingham B5 5TH
Tel: 021–643 8348
Information, advice and friendly support for widows, particularly helping them to overcome the problems of loneliness, isolation and financial difficulties.

See also 'Help and Friendship' (page 54).

ELDERLY ABUSE

It is estimated that up to 10 per cent of elderly people may suffer some form of abuse. This occurs either when the immediate carer is no longer able to care in a loving and sensitive way, or when other family members or visitors to the household may be abusing them.

Abuse may manifest itself in one or a combination of ways:

- physical abuse: hitting, slapping, restraining
- verbal or psychological abuse: blackmail, blaming or swearing
- deprivation: of food, heat, clothing, comfort or cleaning
- forcible isolation: not letting others see or talk to them
- sexual abuse
- misusing medication
- financial abuse: misuse or appropriation of monies or property.

Much abuse of elderly people is the result of carers being stressed, exhausted or isolated. This may happen in one of the following situations:

- when the elderly person has a disability affecting his or her physical, mental or communications performance
- when the person has behavioural or personality disturbances which the carer finds inconsistent and/or hard to understand
- when the family is under stress due to low income or poor housing
- when family relationships are poor or there is a history of violent behaviour.

Elderly abuse is a crime. If you suspect that someone you know is being abused you should contact the Social Services or the police immediately. They will know what action to take and may be able to offer relief to both the carer and the cared for. A leaflet *Abuse of Elderly People* (25p) is available (with sae) from The Distribution Services Department, Age Concern England, 1268 London Road, London SW16 4EJ.

CRIME OR ATTACK

Victim Support
National Office
Cranmer House
39 Brixton Road
London SW9 6DZ
Tel: 071–735 9166
A small number of older people become victims of crime each year, whether through attack or a break-in. Local Victim Support schemes are listed in the telephone book or can be contacted through the local library, Citizens Advice Bureau or Age Concern group.

Victim Support Scotland
7a Royal Terrace
Edinburgh EH2 2HB
Tel: 031–225 7779

VSS is an independent, voluntary organisation offering free practical help, advice, information and emotional support to victims of crime.

POLICY

Centre for Policy on Ageing
Ironmonger Row
London EC1V 3QP
Tel : 071–253 1787
The CPA is an independent organisation that aims to influence public policy affecting the lives of the 13 million older people in the UK. It also seeks to develop and promote policies that will enable people to lead fulfilled lives and maintain independence for as long as possible. The CPA publishes a number of informative leaflets and guides. The following guides refer to care issues:
Community Life: A Code of Practice for Community Care (£6)
Caring by Day: A Study of Day Care Services for Older People (£11)

Food, Glorious Food: A Review of Meals Services for Older People (£7)
Caring for Cash: The Issue of Private Domiciliary Care (£6.50)
Continuing Care Communities: A Viable Option in Britain (£7.50)

The British Pensioner and Trade Union Action Association (BPTAA)
Norman Dodds House
315 Bexley Road
Erith
Kent DA8 3EZ
Tel: 0322 335464
The BPTAA works to encourage pensioners to support improvements in provisions made for older people.

HELP AND FRIENDSHIP

The Association of Jewish Friendship Clubs for the Over-60s
Woburn House
Upper Woburn Place
London WC1
Tel: 071–387 8980
The Association forms friendship clubs for the over-60s to alleviate loneliness and to provide friendship and activities.

The British Association for Service to the Elderly
119 Hassell Street
Newcastle under Lyme
Staffs ST5 1AX
Tel: 0782 661033

This organisation provides opportunities for professional or private carers to meet, talk to others and exchange ideas.

Age-Link
9 Narborough Close
Brackenbury Village
Ickenham
Middlesex UB1D 8TN
Tel: 081–571 5324
Age-Link aims to befriend lonely or housebound elderly people by arranging outings on a Sunday afternoon once a month, often to the homes of other Age-Link members.

National Association of Women's Clubs

5 Vernon Rise
King's Cross Road
London WC1X 9EP
Tel: 071–837 1434
For information about what clubs are available locally.

Contact

15 Henrietta Street
Covent Garden
London WC2E 8QH
Tel: 071–240 0630
Contact aims to provide companion-ship and regular outings within a Contact group of elderly people who live alone without family support and who are no longer able to get out without assistance.

Lewisham Pensioners Link

74 Deptford High Street
London SE8 4RT
Tel: 081–691 0938
Lewisham Pensioners Link is a London-based group which arranges projects for pensioners, as well as offering friendship and home help, health advice and information, welfare rights assistance and physical help to keep out the cold. Contact them to find out more or to locate local branches.

Elders Voice

Carlton Centre
Granville Road
London NW6 2BX
Tel: 071–624 3480
For pensioners in the Brent area.

Sixty Plus

7 Thorpe Close
London W10 5XL
Tel: 081–969 9105

For pensioners in the Kensington and Chelsea areas.

In addition, Sixty Plus runs a 'Cold-line'—a hypothermia prevention 24-hour emergency line which gives advice and referrals for heating repairs and draughtproofing. Information from:
Coldline
31 Dalston Lane
London E8 3DF
Tel: 071–241 0440

The Distressed Gentlefolks Aid Association

Vicarage Gate House
Vicarage Gate
London W8 4AQ
Tel: 071–229 9341
DGAA makes regular allowances and emergency grants for those of profes-sional and similar backgrounds who find themselves in need or distress. These grants sometimes are made in conjunction with other charities and are designed to help beneficiaries stay in their own homes. In addition, the Association runs 13 homes around England. Some of these provide resi-dential care for the elderly; others provide more intensive nursing care. Entry conditions can be checked with head office.

The National Association of Leagues of Hospital Friends

Second Floor
Fairfax House
Causton Road
Colchester
Essex CO1 1RJ
Tel: 0206 761227/761243
The aim of NALHF is to help patients and former patients in hospitals, health care establishments and in the commu-

nity (in both the NHS and private sector) throughout the UK. The range of services includes everything from staffing shops, canteens, libraries and telephone-hotlines to befriending, reception and escort duties, arranging outings, flower arranging, hairdressing, writing letters, finding amenities—the list is endless. Each LHF is autonomous. The national office acts as a support and advice centre to its members and volunteers and provides mail order services, insurance, etc. A wide variety of goods and leaflets are available—catalogue on request.

WHICH CHARITY?

The Association of Charity Officers
c/o RICS Benevolent Fund Ltd
Tavistock House North
Tavistock Square
London WC1H 9RJ
Tel: 071–383 5557
The Association has some 250 members, all of whom are registered charities, giving non-contributory relief and helping people from all walks of life. Its objective is to promote efficiency and encourage co-operation between charities; the Association will try to help enquirers locate possible sources of charitable help.

Charity Search
25 Portview Road
Avonmouth
Bristol BS11 9LD
Tel: 0272 824060
A free advice service that will respond to telephone or written enquiries about helping elderly people in genuine financial difficulties to find established charities that might help them. They publish a book called *Charity Made Clear* (Auriel James; £4.95, send a cheque with every order). The book is written for ordinary people and for those concerned with the welfare of others who are faced with an overwhelming and bewildering mass of charities.

HELP FOR EX-SERVICEMEN AND -WOMEN

**The Forces Help Society and
Lord Roberts Workshops**
122 Brompton Road
London SW3 1JD
Tel: 071–589 3243
The Society helps, according to need, men and women who have served at any time in HM forces, which includes a large proportion of those now elderly, as so many served in the Second World War or did National Service. It provides help to people in need, which includes advice on obtaining benefits and services to which individuals may be entitled. This help is channelled through a network of trained voluntary case-workers organised in co-operation with the Soldiers Sailors Airmen Forces Association. Local contact addresses and telephone numbers may be found at the library or post office and in the telephone directory.

The Society also maintains Cottage Homes for disabled and elderly men and women and their partners. Some of these homes are purpose-built for those suffering from disabilities (not necessarily the result of active service).

The Lord Roberts Workshop provides training and employment for disabled ex-servicemen in Dundee and Edinburgh. They produce a range of goods and furniture.

The Soldiers', Sailors' and Airmen's Families Association
Room 24
19 Queen Elizabeth Street
London SE1 2IP
Tel: 071–403 8783
This charitable organisation aids the widows and families of ex-servicemen.

The British Limbless Ex-Servicemen's Association (BLESMA)
185–187 High Road
Chadwell Heath
Romford
Essex RM6 6NA
Tel: 081–590 1124
BLESMA provides visits to check on the welfare of members and their widows and a counselling service. It has permanent residential and respite care homes at Blackpool and Creiff and provides advice on pensions and allowances; it also represents members at Appeal Tribunals. It provides financial assistance in the form of grants, and offers limited funding for research and development in the field of prosthetics and orthotics. BLESMA also

acts as a consumer watchdog in respect of artificial limbs, wheelchairs and appliances, and has a nationwide branch structure. Publications include:
Better Health for the Amputee (75p)
Out on a Limb (£2)
Driving after Amputation (50p)
How to Get Back Behind the Wheel (50p)
BLESMAG—in house journal (published three times a year, £1)

Royal British Legion
48 Pall Mall
London SW1Y 5JY
Tel: 071–973 0633
The Royal British Legion promotes the welfare of service and ex-service men and women and their dependents, relieving hardship where it exists.

The War Widows Association of Great Britain
17 The Earl's Croft
Coventry, CV3 5ES
Tel: 0203 503298
The Association was founded to improve conditions for war widows and their families. It works with other ex-service and service organisations including the Central Committee on War Pensions. It has about 50 regional organisers throughout Britain, who contact members via letters, meetings and a thrice-yearly newsletter.

HELP FOR DISABLED PEOPLE

The Disabled Living Foundation
380–384 Harrow Road
London W9 2HU
Tel: 071–289 6111
The DLF was established in 1970 to serve people with special physical

needs by providing practical advice and information on all aspects of independent living. The DLF's professional advisers respond to some 30,000 enquiries each year, mainly on equipment for disabled people. A large number of specialist publications are available on many subjects including health, equipment, clothing and shoes: for a publications list send sae.

The British Red Cross Society
9 Grosvenor Crescent
London SW1X 7EJ
Tel: 071–235 5454
The British Red Cross provides a range of services throughout the UK, including medical loans and mobility aids, an escort and transport service, therapeutic beauty care and domiciliary services. It also operates an international tracing and message service, first aid duties and training and, in parts of the UK, a home from hospital scheme and day care services.

The Physically Handicapped and Able Bodied (PHAB) (England)
12–14 London Road
Croydon CR0 2TA
Tel: 081–667 9443

PHAB Northern Ireland
25 Alexandra Gardens
Belfast BT15 3LJ
Tel: 0232 370240

PHAB Scotland
Princes House
5 Shandwick Place
Edinburgh EH2 4RG
Tel: 031–229 3559

PHAB Wales
First Floor
179 Penarth Road
Cardiff CF1 7JW
Tel: 0222 223677
PHAB exists to further the integration of people with and without disabilities. This is done through over 500 clubs throughout the UK.

RADAR (Royal Association for Disability and Rehabilitation)
25 Mortimer Street
London W1N 8AB
Tel: 071–637 5400
RADAR is a national organisation working with and for physically disabled people to remove architectural, economic and attitudinal barriers. RADAR is particularly involved in the areas of education, employment, mobility, health, social services, housing and access. The association produces a number of publications and operates in conjunction with an affiliated network of over 500 local and national organisations.

RADAR offers a large number of publications. For prices and details, send for a publications list. Subjects covered include: access, education, employment, health services, holidays, housing, legal and parliamentary matters, mobility and travel, national key scheme, Social Security and finances, Social Services and community living, sport and leisure.

VOLUNTEERS

Many organisations desperately need volunteers to help with fundraising, home visits, even organising community work—the activities are numerous. Voluntary work can be enormously rewarding and a good means of keeping active and meeting people.

Listed below are just few of the organisations that welcome volunteers. Older people could contact their favourite charity to offer their services or go to their Citizens Advice Bureau, library, church or hospital.

Community Service Volunteers

237 Pentonville Road
London N1 9NG
Tel: 071–278 6601
CSV's Retired and Senior Volunteer Programme (RSVP—see below) harnesses the skills and experience of older people to enrich schools, hospitals and community projects and to help protect the environment. Older volunteers use their business experience to advise younger people starting out on their own. Younger full-time volunteers work face-to-face with older people, helping them to live independently in their own homes.

Retired and Senior Volunteer Programme (RSVP)

237 Pentonville Road
London N1 9NG
Tel: 071–278 6601
RSVP aims to encourage anyone 50+ to participate in volunteering. It recognises the skills of older people and provides group commitment and support. The programme is for anyone over 50 who wants to be involved in the community. Each group plans its own activities, which might include working with elderly people locally, using business experience to advise young people starting out on their own, or going into primary or secondary schools to help individual pupils or small groups of pupils and support teachers. Free leaflets include: *Your Hidden Talent*.

Women's Royal Voluntary Service (England)

234 Stockwell Road
London SW9 9SP
Tel: 071–416 0146

WRVS Scotland

19 Grosvenor Crescent
Edinburgh EH12 5EL
Tel: 031–337 2261

WRVS Wales

26 Cathedral Road
Cardiff CF1 9LJ
Tel: 0222 228386
Help for elderly people is just part of the range of help supplied by the WRVS: this includes welfare services, care relief holidays, supplies of clothing and bedding, home services and luncheon clubs.

National Association of Volunteer Bureaux

St Peter's College
College Road
Saltley
Birmingham B8 3TE
Tel: 021–327 0265
The National Association of Volunteer Bureaux puts people in touch with their local voluntary agency, which can inform them what volunteer work is available in their area.

Society of Voluntary Associates

Brixton Hill Place
London SW2 1HJ
Tel: 081–671 7833
The SVA recruits and trains volunteers to work with offenders, with projects all over Great Britain.

The National Council for Voluntary Organisations
Regents Wharf
All Saints Street
London N1 9RL
Tel: 071–713 6161

The National Council for Voluntary Organisations supplies information sheets on paid and unpaid work opportunities for people of all ages.

CARING FOR A PET

The Animal Welfare Trust
Tylers Way
Watford By-pass
Watford
Herts WD2 8HQ
Tel: 081–950 8215
The Animal Welfare Trust cares and finds suitable new homes for dogs, cats and other animals which would otherwise be abandoned, left to stray or be put to sleep. No healthy animal is put to sleep however long its stay. The Trust recognises the benefits that pets have for the elderly and through its programme Pet Concern provides financial assistance with short-term boarding of senior citizens' pets. The scheme is co-ordinated with the Social Services.

Last year the Trust launched 'Animal Aid for the Elderly' to provide direct help with pets belonging to senior citizens or the physically disabled in cases of illness or emergency. This is provided by a network of voluntary Animal Aiders and co-ordinated through a 24-hour helpline at the Trust's headquarters. It is hoped that many elderly people will feel able to take on pets in the knowledge that the Trust will provide help and advice whenever necessary. Free publications include:
Animal Aid for the Elderly
Emergency Pet Care
Guide to Making a Will

National Canine Defence League
1 Pratt Mews
London NW1 OAD
Tel: 071–388 0137
The NCDL promotes animal ownership for older people and undertakes to find homes for animals whose owners are incapacitated.

The Cinnamon Trust
Poldarves Farm
Trescowe Common
Penzance
Cornwall TR20 9RX
Tel: 0736 850291
This national charity helps elderly and terminally ill people with pets. It offers a fostering service if they have to go into hospital or cannot care for their pet for a while, and will make arrangements for long-term care. In addition, they will help with walking a pet or making visits to the vet if the owner is unable to cope.

People's Dispensary for Sick Animals
Whitechapel Way
Priorslee
Telford
Salop TF2 9PQ
Tel: 0952 290999
The People's Dispensary for Sick Animals will help people who cannot afford vets' fees—the level of assistance is means-tested by the amount of

Income Support, Family Credit or
Housing Benefit one is receiving.

Canine Concern Scotland Trust
East Lodge
Caldarvan
Gartocharn
Strathclyde
Tel: 0389 83325
Volunteers from this agency will assist
dog owners who fall ill.

Further Reading
Age and Vulnerability: A Guide to Better Care, Olive Stevenson (Edward Arnold, 1989), £8.25
   Care for The Carer, Christine Orton (Thorsons, 1989), £4.99
   Caring at Home, Nancy Kohner (King's Fund Informal Caring Programme, 1988), £3
   Caring for Parents in Later Life, Avril Rodway (Consumers Association, 1992), £9.95
   Coping with Ageing Parents, Chris Gilleard and Glenda Watt (W & R Chambers, 1983), £3.95
   Counselling Carers—Supporting Relatives of Confused Elderly People at Home, Andrew Papadopoulos (Winslow Press, 1990), £6.95
   Handbook for Care Assistants: A Practical Guide for Carers (Scottish Action on Dementia, 1991), £3 (approx)
   Loneliness: How to Overcome It, Val Marriott and Terry Timblick (Age Concern England, 1988), £3.95

chapter four

WHERE TO LIVE

Adapting Your Parents' Home or Helping Them Find a
Suitable Alternative, Care and Nursing Services at Home

WHILE RESEARCHING THIS BOOK I came across the widest possible spectrum of older people, from the 96-year old lady who lives happily and successfully on her own to the merchant banker in his early sixties with Alzheimer's Disease who requires full nursing care.

While no two situations are ever exactly the same, certain criteria do exist to help you assess where it would be best for your older parents or relatives to live. This involves the rest of the family answering certain questions:

- How capable is the older person (or persons) concerned?
- Can they look after themselves: cooking, hygiene, security, taking medication when necessary?
- Can they look after their house and garden?
- Can they get out and about: to the doctor, on visits, holidays, for leisure activities?
- How suitable is their current accommodation in terms of:
  size and manageability
  accessibility (stairs, ramps) and
  potential for adaptation

  location (proximity to neighbours, family, shops)
- Do they have any special needs now (or will they have in the foreseeable future) concerning:
  company (i.e. loneliness)
  finance
  provision of food
  health
  looking after the house, repairs and maintenance?
- Has the future ever been discussed in terms of where they will live if they become less able to cope on their own?

It is remarkable how seldom this last question has ever been broached within families so that, when the time comes, there has been no preparation or consideration of finances, location or type of accommodation, and certainly no visits made to compare the alternatives before a decision *has* to be made.

Usually the decision has to be made quickly, more often than not prompted by an accident or illness which leaves older persons unable to look after themselves as competently as before, sometimes after a stay in hospital. Lack of advance preparation could mean a hasty decision or a series of moves until the right place is available, which might make the whole process far more traumatic than it need be.

THE ALTERNATIVES

Two broad accommodation options exist for older people:
1. Adapting their existing home so that it is more suitable for advancing years (see 'Staying Put', below).
2. Moving to alternative accommodation: sheltered housing or a residential or nursing home (page 68).

STAYING PUT

There is no doubt that older people should be encouraged to continue to live in their own home for as long as possible. There is no substitute for the surroundings, friends, neighbours and neighbourhood with which they are familiar.

Local Authority grants may be available to assist with adaptation work but individuals will be means-tested according to the type of grant required and the circumstances of the applicant. It is important to obtain agreement from the Authority before proceeding with any alterations. Applicants should contact the renovation grants section of their local council, who will be able to suggest what sort of grant to apply for.

The Social Fund, which is run by the Benefits Agency, provides grants and loans for people on Income Support. Older people may be able to get help with repairs by applying for a Community Care Grant. Any savings over £1000 (£500 if the applicants are under 60) will be taken into account. Leaflets SB16 *A Guide to the Social Fund* and SFL2 *How the Social Fund Can Help You* are available free from Benefits Agency offices.

Disabled facilities grants are available for disabled tenants and owner-occupiers to adapt their homes so that they can manage more independently—applicants should contact the renovations grants section at their local council.

A number of organisations exist to assist with the process of adapting homes and helping with the cost, both in terms of physical changes and the use of additional local services in order that older homeowners may stay in their homes. These agencies run the adaptation schemes and can give advice about building repairs, adaptations and costs, as well as about any loans or grants that may be available. Some of the agencies arrange and supervise the building work: Care and Repair Ltd was chosen to be the national co-ordinating body for all home improvement agencies and so can identify providers all over the country.

Central enquiries:

Care and Repair Ltd (England)
22a The Ropewalk
Nottingham NG1 5DT
Tel: 0602 799091

Care and Repair Scotland
Fifth Floor
Mercantile Chambers
53 Boswell Street
Glasgow G2 6TS
Tel: 041–248 7177

Care and Repair Cymru Ltd
Norbury House
Norbury Road
Cardiff CF5 3AS
Tel: 0222 576286

Other organisations that can help to identify repairs or adaptations that need to be carried out or considered and that can recommend contractors and assist with loans are:

Anchor
Anchor House
269a Banbury Road
Oxford OX2 7HU
Tel: 0865 311511

Northern Ireland Housing Executive
The Housing Centre
2 Adelaide Street
Belfast BT2 8PB
Tel: 0232 240588

Orbit Housing Association
23 Ewell Road
Cheam
Surrey SM3 8DD
Tel: 081–661 9921
(phone for local regional office)

The Centre
The Centre is the only UK charity whose role is to help ensure that buildings are convenient and safe for all users, including disabled and elderly people. The Centre is an information and training resource for the construction industry, the care profession and disabled and elderly people and their families. The Centre can advise on how to make a house or flat more comfortable and convenient, publishes design guidance, and can put people in touch with experienced architects in their locality.

The Centre for Accessible Environments
35 Great Smith Street
London SW1P 3BJ
Tel: 071–222 7980
The Centre also offers information and advice on the design and technical matters to be considered in order to accommodate all types of people, including the elderly and disabled.

Care in the Community

The Government's new community care approach, 'Care in the Community' came into effect on 1 April 1993, and is all about assessing older people's need for help and helping them either to remain in their own home for as long as they are willing and able or to move to residential or nursing accommodation. Different people need different kinds of help and a range of services can enable them to stay in their own homes, for example meals on wheels or home help (see Chapter 3, page 51), and help with repairs, improvements or adaptations to the home.

Who Can Help?

If your parent or relative needs help or assistance of any kind you should telephone your local Social Services Department, or Social Work Department in Scotland, for further information or assessment of the help you might need (phone number in the telephone book under the name of your local council). Local authority grants towards the cost of repair and maintenance may be available, but they are means-tested and are dependent on the local authority's own resources.

For advice on Care in the Community, and how it affects Attendance Allowance, Disability Living Allowance and Housing Benefit you can contact Freeline Social Security on 0800 666555 or contact your local Benefits Agency office.

All sorts of equipment is available to make life easier around the home. Stairlifts, bath seats, handrails—further details are given in Chapter 8.

Local Citizens Advice Bureaux and the Department of Social Security also provide a wealth of information as to additional services available. If required, a social worker will visit at home to discuss and advise about any services that might be needed. These may include:

- home help
- laundry service
- waste disposal
- meals on wheels
- district nurses
- day centres.

See also Chapter 1, page 21.

Homelife DGAA
Vicarage Gate
Kensington
London W8 4AQ
Tel: 071–229 9341

Homelife is a charity which gives financial help to people to either stay in their homes, including assistance with bills, equipment and repairs, or help to go into nursing homes.

Further useful information may be obtained from:

Shelter—National Campaign for Homeless People
88 Old Street
London EC1V 9HU
Tel: 071–253 0202

Shelter provides free, confidential advice through a network of Housing Aid Centres to people experiencing housing problems.

Community Service Volunteers along with RSVP (its Retired and Senior Volunteer Programme) can offer help to people in their own homes in terms of help, care and visits (see page 59 for the address).

The local Age Concern Group will be able to advise special services in the area which they or other groups run. In addition, it publishes *Your Rights* (£1.95), which gives information about Social Security benefits and other sources of financial help, including retirement pension, disability benefits and income-related benefits (see page 48 for the address).

Capital Release

Several companies assist retired homeowners with capital release, enabling them to raise a tax-free lump sum against their property. This allows them to continue to live in their home with guaranteed occupancy; the money can be spent to increase their standard of living, pay for home improvements, buy a holiday or be invested in any way. As with any financial undertaking, arrangements with any such company should be supervised by a solicitor (see page 132).

Age Alliance
6 Allerton Hill
Leeds LS7 3QB
Tel: 0532 370666
The Age Alliance Home Reversion Plan assists retired homeowners to raise a tax-free lump sum *without risk* by selling part or all of their property equity. They continue to live in their own home and receive guaranteed lifetime occupancy arranged through their own solicitor. There are no repayments

or interest. The money can be spent or invested in any way.

Home and Capital Trust Ltd
31 Goldington Road
Bedford, MK40 3LH
Tel: 0234 340511
Home and Capital Trust allows capital release, with a cash lump sum, through the sale of all or part of the property, while retaining a lifetime rent-free occupancy.

Care and Nursing Services at Home

Hundreds of independent organisations throughout the UK provide social or nursing care for older or disabled people in their own homes. There are licensed employment and/or nursing agencies as well as charitable or voluntary organisations. The fees will vary according to the duties and hours involved, and you should check the agency's charges (including commission, VAT, joining fee) and its code of practice before making a commitment.

Government policy suggests that home care services are to become the preferred approach of community care and that a 'mixed economy of care' should be promoted. A responsible and effective independent body, The United Kingdom Home Care Association (UKHCA), has been formed to speak for the independent providers and raise the profile of home care services generally with its 'UKHCA Code of Practice'. A recommended complaints procedure is now available. The Association's representatives work closely with colleagues in the public sector. For further information:

The United Kingdom Home Care Association
c/o 22 Southway
Carshalton
Surrey SM5 4HW
Tel: 081–770 3658 (Please note: this is expected to change early in 1994)

Cleshar Community Care
108 Fortis Green Road
London N10 3HN
Tel: 081–444 0954
Cleshar provides a home care nursing service as well as supplying staff to Social Services, National Health hospitals and private establishments. Cleshar will visit people at home, without obligation, to assess and discuss individual needs and compile a tailor-made plan of care, including a financial assessment of the situation.

Somerset Care Ltd
Acacia House
Swingbridge
Bathpool
Taunton
Somerset TA2 8BY
Tel: 0823 323584
Somerset Care can supply home care and a range of domestic services for people needing help throughout Somerset and in neighbouring counties, along with community services, laundry, meals, day care short stays and residential care.

British Nursing Association
North Place
82 Great North Road
Hatfield
Herts AL9 5BL
Tel: 0707 263544
The British Nursing Association provides fully qualified nurses, carers or auxiliaries to private patients in their own homes.

Care Alternatives
206 Worple Road
Wimbledon
London SW20 8PN
Tel: 081–946 8202
Care Alternatives introduces reliable caring staff to elderly or disabled people to undertake such tasks as cooking and shopping, or they can provide full clinical nursing expertise, residential nursing, and other specialist services such as occupational therapy. Write or telephone for further details and rates.

Country Cousins Employment Bureau
10a Market Square
Horsham
W. Sussex RH12 1EX
Country Cousins is a company which can supply temporary residential helpers who have some form of nursing background for the general care of people during family crises, illness or convalescence.

Other Nursing Agencies

Anzac Nursing Services
297 Kings Road
London SW3 5EP
Tel: 071–352 2383

Independent Home Care Nursing Services
596 High Road
Woodford Green
IG8 0PS
Tel: 081–504 1038

SMD Agency
37 Taylors Crescent
Cranleigh
Surrey GU6 7EN
Tel: 0483 274085

MOVING TO ALTERNATIVE ACCOMMODATION

The choice here is dependent upon the level of support required. There are three distinct accommodation options, each of which is supplied by both the private and public sectors, as well as some which are aided or funded by charitable or voluntary organisations. These are:
1. sheltered housing
2. residential care homes
3. nursing homes.

Sheltered Housing

Sheltered housing involves a collection of apartments or bungalows within a defined and protected area offering a degree of privacy and some communal facilities. These are provided by councils, housing associations and private developers and are available to rent or buy.

Residences are self-contained and are generally unfurnished—residents are encouraged to bring their own furnishings. There is usually a warden on duty to oversee residents and there may be a communal laundry, common room, or dining room: services differ from scheme to scheme. Sheltered housing is usually conveniently located for shops and other local facilities.

Be sure to check not only the rent or purchase price, but also the service charges that cover facilities and services such as provision of a warden, laundry facilities, alarm systems, home and garden maintenance, etc. Some developers offer schemes by which a person is offered housing at a discount in return for the ownership of the property when that person dies. *You should always take independent legal and financial advice before making any commitment.*

It is also important to check the maintenance and service charges before committing. Any complaints or queries about service charges, maintenance, etc. should be addressed to the Sheltered Housing Advisory and Conciliation Service on 071–383 2006, which is staffed by Age Concern.

The local Social Services Department or Age Concern group (address and telephone numbers on page 50) should know if there are any sheltered housing schemes in your or your parent's area for sale or rent.

Age Concern England also produces a free factsheet: *Sheltered Housing For Sale* (address page 48).

Help the Aged produces an information sheet: *Sheltered Housing* (address page 49). Counsel and Care also produces a factsheet: *Special Accommodation for Older People* (25p) (address page 49).

The Elderly Accommodation Counsel
46a Chiswick High Road
London W4 1SZ
Tel: 081–995 8320
The Counsel maintains a national central database of all types of private and voluntary accommodation suitable to meet the needs of those over the age of retirement, including sheltered housing and homes and hospices. The charity conducts an ongoing programme into the medical acceptance criteria for entry into such types of accommodation together with details and statistics on costs. Information can also be given on sources of top-up funding.

The National Association of Estate Agents
Arbon House
21 Jury Street
Warwick CV34 4EH
Tel: 0926 496800
The NAEA can offer free referral to anyone wishing to buy or sell property in another town or district through its National Homelink Service.

A large number of private schemes, charitable and housing trusts and housing associations do exist. A few are listed below:

The Abbeyfield Society
186–192 Darkes Lane
Potters Bar
Herts EN6 1AB
Tel: 0707 644845
The Abbeyfield Society provides 'very sheltered' rental housing for older people within their chosen community. Abbeyfield Houses strive to be non-institutional and care is given in family-type houses, built or adapted in accordance with statutory requirements. Residents have their own room which they can furnish with their own belongings. Abbeyfield 'supportive' houses have resident housekeepers, and 'extra care' houses provide 24-hour personal care for frail older people. Abbeyfield has a range of literature—further details on request.

The New Homes Marketing Board
82 Cavendish Street
London W1M 8AD
Tel: 071–580 5588
NHMB offers a list of companies which are offering sheltered housing for sale.

McCarthy and Stone
Homelife House
26–32 Oxford Road
Bournemouth BH8 8EZ
Tel: 0202 292480
MacCarthy and Stone owns and operates comfortable, secure retirement

flats and homes with security alarms, communal laundry facilities, house managers and maintenance teams. Further details and rates on request.

The North British Housing Association

4 The Pavilions
Portway
Preston
Lancs PR2 2YB
Tel: 0772 897200

One of the country's leading housing associations, North British provides a range of good quality, affordable housing for older people, including carefully designed warden-assisted flats and bungalows, sheltered accommodation and 'housing with care' schemes for frail elderly people. It is a non-profit making organisation, active in most parts of the country.

Castle Rock Housing Association Ltd

2 Wishaw Terrace
Meadowbank
Edinburgh EH7 6AF
Tel: 031–652 0152

Retirement Lease Housing Association

19 Eggars Court
St George's Road East
Aldershot
Hants GU12 4LN
Tel: 0252 318181

This company offers sheltered housing is sites in Hampshire and Sussex.

Community Home Care

Arkley Nursing Home
Barnet Road
Barnet
Herts EN5 3LJ
Tel: 081–441 7272

Community Home Care owns and operates retirement homes, hospitals and nursing homes throughout the UK. Its Orchard Lea development is a new concept of 'close care' which allows older people to buy a home; all insurance, maintenance, light, heat and even some cooking are covered by the monthly service charge. A 24-hour emergency call is in operation and other assistance may be called upon as needed.

The Country Houses Association

41 Kingsway
London WC2B 6UB
Tel: 071–836 1624

This company has converted nine historic mansions into apartments which are available for sale.

The Humanist Housing Association

311 Kentish Town Road
London NW5 2TJ
Tel: 071–485 8776

The HHA provides sheltered accommodation for older people with proven need for help.

The English Courtyard Association

8 Holland Street
London W8 4LT
Tel: 071–937 3890

This association sells two- and three-bedroomed country cottages with garden (and gardener) offering privacy, security and freedom.

Sheltered Housing Services Ltd
8–9 Abbey Parade
London W5 1EE
Tel: 081–997 9313
SHS operates an up-to-date national
register of privately-owned sheltered
housing for sale throughout the UK.

The Selby Trust
Weston House
Weston Road
Southend
Essex SS1 1AS
Tel: 0702 291127

Housing Associations
For information on properties available for sale or rent through local authorities, voluntary organisations and special schemes, the following housing associations can be contacted:

**The National Federation of
Housing Associations**
175 Gray's Inn Road
London WC1X 8UP
Tel: 071–278 6571

**The Scottish Federation of Housing
Associations**
38 York Place
Edinburgh EH1 3HU
Tel: 031–556 5777

**The Welsh Federation of Housing
Associations**
Norbury House
Norbury Road
Fairwater
Cardiff CF5 3AS
Tel: 0222 555022

**The Northern Ireland Federation of
Housing Associations**
88 Clifton Street
Belfast BT13 1AB
Tel: 0232 230446

Astra Housing Association
Refuge House
64 Stuart Street
Luton
Beds LU1 2SW
Tel: 0582 429398

**The Five Counties Housing
Association Ltd**
Three Counties House
Festival Way
Stoke on Trent ST1 5PX
Tel: 0782 219200

Heritage Housing Ltd
36 Albany Street
Edinburgh
EH1 3QH
Tel: 031–557 0598

Kirk Care Housing Association
3 Forres Street
Edinburgh EH3 6BJ
Tel: 031–225 7246

Methodist Homes for the Aged
Epworth House
Stuart Street
Derby DE1 2EQ
Tel: 0332 296200

Nationwide Housing Trust
Moulton Park
Northampton NN3 1NL
Tel: 0604 794189

North Housing
Ridley House
Regent Centre
Newcastle upon Tyne NE3 3JE
Tel: 091–285 0311

Northern Counties Homes
Princes Buildings
Oxford Court
Oxford Street
Manchester M2 3WQ
Tel: 061–228 3388

Northern Ireland Co-ownership Housing Association Ltd
Murray House
Murray Street
Belfast BT1 6DN
Tel: 0232 327276

Presbyterian Housing Association Northern Ireland Ltd
Lowry House
27 Hampton Park
Belfast
Tel: 0232 491851

The Shires Housing Association Ltd
Three Counties House
Festival Way
Stoke on Trent ST1 5PZ
Tel: 0782 219200

The Sutton Housing Trust
Sutton Court
Tring
Herts HP23 5BB
Tel: 0442 891100

Hanover Housing Association
Hanover House
18 The Avenue
Egham
Surrey TW20 9AB
Tel: 0784 438361
A national, non-profit sheltered housing specialist for 30 years, Hanover owns 9000 rented properties across England and manages 4300 more on private estates for sale or rent. Most estates have fully-trained resident managers and all are connected to emergency control centres. Hanover aims to meet the housing and support needs of older people with care, efficiency and economy. Details, including ethnic language leaflets and rates, on request.

Housing Organisations Mobility and Exchange Services (HOMES)
26 Chapter Street
London SW1P 4ND
Tel: 071–233 7077
HOMES is a government organisation which helps people who live in local authority or housing association accommodation to move home, perhaps to be nearer relatives or employment.

Anchor
Anchor House
269a Banbury Road
Oxford OX2 7HU
Tel: 0865 311511
Anchor is a charitable housing trust which provides sheltered housing for those in need all over England. Properties are for sale or rent.

Disabled Housing Trust
Norfolk Lodge
Oakenfield
Burgess Hill
W. Sussex RH15 8SJ
Tel: 0444 239123
The DHT is a charitable trust providing housing (to rent or buy) for the physically handicapped.

Church of Ireland Housing Association (Northern Ireland) Ltd
74 Dublin Road
Belfast BT2 7HP
Tel: 0232 242130

Derwent Housing Association Ltd
Phoenix Street
Derby DE1 2ER
Tel: 0332 46477

English Churches Housing Group
Sutherland House
70–78 West Hendon Broadway
London NW9 7BT
Tel: 081–203 9233

Fold Housing Association
3 Redburn Square
Holywood
Co. Down, BT18 9HZ
Tel: 0232 428314

Friends of the Elderly and Gentlefolks Help
42 Ebury Street
London SW1W 0LZ
Tel: 071–730 8263

Guardian Housing Association Ltd
Anchor House
269a Banbury Road
Oxford OX2 7HU
Tel: 0865 311711

The Guinness Trust
17 Mendy Street
High Wycombe
Bucks HP11 2NZ
Tel: 0494 535823

James Butcher Housing Association
39 High Street
Theale
Reading RG7 5AH
Tel: 0734 323434

Jephson Homes Housing Association Ltd
Jephson House
Blackdown
Leamington Spa
Warwicks CV32 6RE
Tel: 0926 339311

Merseyside Improved Homes
46 Wavertree Road
Liverpool L7 1PH
Tel: 051–709 9375

Retirement Lease Housing Association
19 Eggar's Court
St George's Road
Aldershot
Hants GU12 4LN
Tel: 0252 318181

Royal Air Forces Association
Portland Road
Malvern
Worcs WR14 2TA
Tel: 0684 892505

**The Royal British Legion Housing
Association Ltd**
PO Box 32
St John's Road
Penn
High Wycombe
Bucks HP10 8JF
Tel: 0494 813771

Hadleigh Retirement Homes
Highfield House
27 South Street
Tarring
Worthing BN14 7LG
Tel: 0903 204106

Select Retirement
Manor View Offices
Ringwood Road
Burley
Hants BH24 4BR
Tel: 0425 403777

Further Reading
A Buyer's Guide to Sheltered Housing, Age Concern England (Central Books),
£2.50
   Retirement Homes and Finance is a bi-monthly magazine available from
newsagents, priced £1.30.

Residential Homes and Nursing Homes

Residential or care homes are for people who, although still fairly independent,
do require some assistance (perhaps with washing, dressing or cooking). Residents
are generally encouraged to bring some of their own belongings when they move
in. When considering a home it is important to check that it is near to shops and
other facilities so that the resident's sense of independence may be maintained.

By law any private or voluntary residential care home with four or more residents has to be registered with the Local Authority Social Services Department.

The Relatives Association was founded in March 1992 for the relatives and
friends of elderly people in all types of residential care, nursing homes and long-
stay hospitals. It aims to provide a framework nationally (and eventually, locally),
through which relatives can work together to maintain and improve the quality
of residential care for older people and to assist in creating common understanding between staff, relatives and residents. A newsletter is circulated quarterly and deals with varied topics such as procedure, guilt and Government policy.
A publication, *Relative Views*, is available on request. For further information
contact:

The Relatives Association
Twyman House
16 Bonny Street
London NW1 9PG
Tel: 071–284 2541/081–201 9153

Nursing homes are residential or care homes which provide 24-hour nursing cover. They must be run by a qualified doctor or nurse and are more suitable for people who need constant attention from trained nurses. By law any home providing nursing care to more than one person has to be registered with the District Health Authority.

How to Choose a Residential or Nursing Home
About three quarters of the 14,000 residential care homes in the UK are run by private or voluntary organisations, the rest by local authorities. Fees in the run-for-profit homes vary enormously and before committing to a particular home it is vital to check and compare not only the facilities, but also the projected fee increases over the next few years.

How to choose the right residential care home for someone you love? Choosing a residential home is a decision which should be made jointly and carefully. Here are a few of the factors to consider when deciding:

- *Visitors.* Are you and other visitors made welcome? Good homes operate an open-door policy whereby visitors are made welcome, within the limitations of meal- and bedtimes.
- *Level of care.* Is the level of care offered suitable and/or adequate? If continual care is required because of illness, disability or frailness then a nursing home registered with the Local Health Authority is needed. More active elderly persons are recommended to a Residential Care Home registered with the Social Services Department (or Social Work Department in Scotland). Some homes have dual registration, which ensures residents a home even if they do become frail and in need of continuous care.
- *Personal Relationships.* On your exploratory visits try to observe the relationship between residents and staff: Is it friendly and happy?
- *Physical Needs.* Are there aids to mobility and independence to help residents as they become less mobile and steady?
- *Independence and Privacy.* Can residents choose at what time they rise and retire? Do they have freedom or are their movements regimented?—it is important that they maintain their independence.
- *Location.* Is the home near to where you or other relatives live? Is it near to public transport and other amenities and shops to help make your visits there easier and so that your relative may get out and about?
- *Happiness.* No amount of physical care can substitute for happiness and homeliness. Talk to other residents and see whether they seem completely comfortable and happy.

Who Pays?

The Government's new community care arrangements have meant changes to the Income Support available for people going into residential care or nursing homes. If your relative needs financial help to enter a residential care or nursing home you must first contact your local authority's Social Services Department (Social Work Department in Scotland). They will discuss the most suitable type of care and, if appropriate, find your relative a place in a home or help you choose one. The Department will pay the home's fees and will work out how much your relative can afford to contribute, based on income, benefits and capital. He or she will also be allowed a personal expenses allowance.

Further information can be obtained from Freeline Social Security on 0800 666555. Leaflet IS50, *Help If You Live in a Residential Care Home or Nursing Home* is available from local Benefits Agency offices.

Age Concern England (address page 48) produces a free factsheet, *Finding Residential and Nursing Home Accommodation*. Help the Aged (address page 49) publishes an information sheet, *Residential and Nursing Homes*, which details how to choose and how to pay for one. Counsel and Care (address page 49) produces *Finding Suitable Residential and Nursing Accommodation* (London only) (10p).

Further Reading

At Home in a Home, Pat Young (Age Concern, 1988), £3.95

Directory of Residential Care Facilities in Scotland, Margaret Scott (ed.) (Scottish Council for Voluntary Organisations, 1989), £7.50

Laing's Review of Private Health Care 1992/93 and Directory of Independent Hospitals, Residential and Nursing Homes and Related Services (Laing and Buisson, 1993), £35

The Daily Telegraph Guide to Living and Retiring Abroad, Mike Furnell (Kogan Page Ltd, 6th edition, 1992), £8.99

How to Find a Private Nursing Home or a Private or Voluntary Residential Care Home

Your local Age Concern group, Citizens Advice Bureau and Community Health Council may offer general advice and lists of residential care or nursing homes in the area.

The Registration Officer for Private Nursing Homes will be able to give a list of private homes in your area. Contact the District Health Authority (address in the telephone book).

The Registered Nursing Home Association
Calthorpe House
Hagley Road
Edgbaston
Birmingham B16 8QY
Tel: 021–454 2511
The Registered Nursing Home Association publishes a directory of nursing homes which reach certain high standards. They can also give details of homes in particular areas.

Independent Health Care Association
22 Little Russell Street
London WC1A 2HT
Tel: 071–430 0537
The Independent Health Care Association is the representative body for independent hospitals, psychiatric hospitals and nursing and residential homes.

Other sources of information to help you to choose a residential care or nursing home are:

- Personal recommendation
  If someone knows a particular home this can be the best way to make a choice.
- Yellow Pages
  Look under Residential and Retirement Homes or Nursing Homes. Make sure you visit several and use the checklist at the beginning of this chapter (page 62) before making a choice.
- Social workers
  Based at the Social Services Department (or Social Work Department in Scotland), or, if your relative is in hospital, the hospital itself may be able to provide a list of homes and general advice.
- Counsel and Care for the Elderly
  This charity visits private residential and nursing homes in the London area and can provide a list of homes as well as a general advisory service (address page 49).

The Directory of Independent Hospitals and Health Services
Longman Group UK Ltd
Fourth Avenue
Harlow
Essex CM19 5AA
Tel: 0279 429655
This directory details all the independent hospitals and health services, voluntary and private rest and nursing homes. The directory costs £92 or is available at reference libraries.

GRACE
35 Walnut Tree Close
Guildford
Surrey GU1 4UL
Tel: 0483 304354
A private organisation offering experienced, sympathetic advice on all aspects of care for older people. Carefully assessed information is kept about residential homes, nursing homes and nursing agencies throughout the country. Registration with GRACE costs £25 or £75 for a personal consultation in your own home.

The British Federation of Care Home Proprietors
852 Melton Road
Thurmaston
Leicester LE4 8BN
Tel: 0533 640095
The BFCHP promotes professional standards in the delivery of quality care and advises on selection of residential and nursing care. Leaflets include *How to Choose a Care Home*, free with sae.

John Groom's Association for the Disabled
10 Gloucester Drive
Finsbury Park
London N4 2LP
Tel: 081–802 7272
This Association runs projects to help disabled people, including residential and holiday accommodation.

The Leonard Cheshire Foundation
26–9 Maunsel Street
London SW1P 2QN
Tel: 071–828 1822
This is a charity which runs residential homes for the disabled and provides part-time care attendants to go into the homes of disabled people.

Somerset Care Ltd
Acacia House
Swingbridge
Bathpool
Taunton
Somerset TA2 8BY
Tel: 0823 323584
Somerset Care owns and operates 26 care and nursing homes in Somerset and neighbouring counties. Details and rates on request.

Two Care
16 Harwood Road
London SW6
Tel: 071–371 0118
Two Care is a charitable housing association with 10 residential and psychiatric rehabilitation homes for people recovering from mental illness.

Ashbourne Homes plc
3 Atlantic Quay
York Street
Glasgow G2 8JH
Tel: 0413 312222

BUPA Care for the Elderly
15 Essex Street
London WC2R 3AX
Tel: 071–379 1111
BUPA provides nursing home care in the UK, with facilities for special needs, diets, hobbies and preferences in short- and long-term, post-operative, respite and terminal care. Rates and details on request.

The Brendoncare Foundation
Brendon
Park Road
Winchester
Hampshire SO23 7BE
Tel: 0962 852133
The Brendoncare Foundation is a not-for-profit organisation and registered charity providing what they call 'Total Care' for older people in residential, nursing and terminal care homes. The homes offer 'security, dignity and a warm, caring atmosphere'.

Fairclough Homes
West Street
Billingshurst
W. Sussex RH14 9ZA
Tel: 0435 865260

Sue Ryder Foundation
Cavendish
Sudbury
Suffolk CO10 8AY
Tel: 0787 280252
The Foundation has over 20 homes in
the UK.

Johansens Care Homes Directory
Freepost
Horsham
W. Sussex RH13 8ZA
Tel: 0800 269397
This is a fully illustrated directory of
independent care homes, many of
which are converted country manors
or similar.

St George's Nursing Home
61 St George's Square
London SW1V 3QR
Tel: 071–821 9001/2
The St George's Nursing home in
London's Victoria offers 24-hour
RGN nursing care in this quiet, residential area with easy access to public
transport and local shopping. Facilities
include an activities room, music
room, television room and day room;
residents are encouraged to bring their
own furnishings and small pets. There
is a visiting service from a hairdresser
and a chiropodist.

The Arkle Lodge Nursing Home
Sprents Lane
Overton
Hants RG25 3HX
Tel: 0256 771353

Takare plc
Takare House
Whitechapel Way
Priorslee
Telford
Salop TF2 9SP
Tel: 0952 292392

Westminster Healthcare plc
48 Leicester Square
London WC2H 7FB
Tel: 071–839 9302

Crestacare Ltd
Cresta House
5 Ambassador Place
Stockport Road
Altrincham
Cheshire WA15 8DB
Tel: 061–927 7099

Court Cavendish Group Ltd
Maple House
2–6 High Street
Potters Bar
Herts EN6 5QR
Tel: 0707 664400

**Country House Retirement Homes
Ltd**
Tannery House
Tannery Lane
Send
Woking
Surrey GU23 7EF
Tel: 0483 211571

Community Hospitals Group plc
Priory Terrace
24 Bromham Road
Bedford MK40 2QD
Tel: 0234 273473

Caledonian Nursing Homes Ltd
St Joseph's Nursing Home
Lochwinnoch
Renfrewshire
Tel: 0505 843390

Sandown Private Nursing Homes
646 Shore Road
Whiteabbey
Co. Antrim BT37 0PR
Tel: 0232 853134

St Andrew's Homes Ltd
35 Grosvenor Place
Jesmond
Newcastle upon Tyne NE2 2RD
Tel: 091–281 6377

Lodge Care plc
Pond Road
Shoreham by Sea
W. Sussex BN43 5WU
Tel: 0273 464724

Northern Caring Homes Ltd
Administration Centre
Winlaton Care Village
Winlaton
Tyne and Wear NE21 6JY
Tel: 091–499 0366

Quality Care Homes Ltd
18–20 St Cuthbert's Way
Darlington
Co Durham DL1 1GB
Tel: 0325 364586

National Care Homes Association
5 Bloomsbury Place
London WC1A 2QA
Tel: 071–436 1871
The National Care Homes Association is a federation of private care homes offering a certain level of standards and advice on anything to do with private residential care.

The Almshouse Association
Billingbear Lodge
Wokingham
Berks RG11 5RU
Tel: 0344 52922
The 2000 UK almshouse charities provide housing for needy, elderly people, usually with previous residence in the area. Vacancies are advertised in the local press and names and addresses of correspondents to almshouse charities may be obtained from the local authority (Housing or Social Services Departments) or the Citizens Advice Bureau. The Almshouse Association is a national charity advising almshouse charities on matters of finance, current legal requirements, standards of accommodation and all aspects of almshouse administration.

Homes for Minorities and Special Needs

Jewish Care
221 Golders Green Road
London NW11 9DW
Tel: 081–458 3282
Jewish Care runs residential and nursing homes and sheltered housing schemes for Jewish people.
There may also be some Asian, Afro-Caribbean or Cypriot housing schemes for frail elderly people in your area—the Social Services Department will be able to help you find out what is available.

Caresearch
c/o United Response
162–164 Upper Richmond Road
London SW15 2SL
Tel: 081–780 9596
Caresearch operates a database which matches the needs of mentally handicapped people with the appropriate residential establishment. There is a fee for this service.

ANS Contract Healthcare
Meadbank
12 Parkgate Road
London SW11 4NN
Tel 071–924 3026
Associated Nursing Services plc works with Health Authorities to provide the best long-term care for the elderly and mentally ill. It is one of the largest operators, with 24 nursing homes and 1200 beds throughout the country. Further details and rates on request.

The Royal National Institute for the Blind
224 Great Portland Street
London W1N 6AA
Tel: 071–388 1266

The RNIB provides high-quality residential care in pleasant surroundings in homes in Harrogate, North Yorks, Westgate-on-Sea, Kent, Burnham-on-Sea, Somerset and Hove.

The Hospice Information Service
St Christopher's Hospice
51–59 Lawrie Park Road
Sydenham
London SE26 6DZ
Tel: 081–778 9252
The Hospice Information Service can give information and advice on hospice and palliative care. Palliative care is the total care of patients with a terminal illness for whom the goal must be the best quality of life for them and their families. Although hospice care is principally for patients with advanced cancer, many hospices will consider applications from patients with other illnesses. There are facilities for in- and out-patients and home care teams. *The Directory of Hospice Services in the UK and Ireland* is available free on receipt of an 11-inch x 9-inch sae with 41p stamp.

Further Information

Age Concern England
Astral House
1268 London Road
London SW16 4ER
Tel: 081–679 8000

Age Concern Scotland
54a Fountainbridge
Edinburgh EH3 9PT
Tel: 031–228 5656

Age Concern Northern Ireland
6 Lower Crescent
Belfast BT7 1NR
Tel: 0232 245729

Age Concern Wales
Fourth Floor
1 Cathedral Road
Cardiff CF1 9SD
Tel: 0222 371566
Most areas have an Age Concern group which provides services, leaflets

and advice. Relevant factsheets include:

Rented Accommodation for Older People

Rented Accommodation for Older People in Greater London

Sheltered Housing for Sale

Finding Residential and Nursing Home Accommodation

Local Authorities and Residential Care

Age Concern also publishes a book, *Housing Options for Older People* (£4.95)

Counsel and Care for the Elderly

Twyman House
16 Bonny Street
London NW1 9PG
Tel: 071–485 1566 (Monday, Tuesday, Thursday and Friday, 10.30 a.m. to 4 p.m.)

Counsel and Care visits establishments and has a list of available resources. Relevant publications (free unless otherwise indicated) include:

From Home to A Home (1992), £5

Special Accommodation for Older People (1992)

What to Look for in a Private or Voluntary Registered Home

Help at Home

Finding Suitable Residential and Nursing Accommodation (London only)

Community Care Services for Older People

chapter five

HOLIDAYS

Financing Them, Enjoying Them—All the Options

THESE DAYS THE CHOICE of holidays is fantastic. Practically every country in the world is accessible: there are hotels, villas and apartments to stay in; sporting, adventure, camping, hobby and health holidays; rail, coach, fly-drive, group travel or 'solo' holidays; stays in one place or multi-centre holidays—the list is endless.

Travel agents are there to advise people of every interest, ability or disability about what is available and what would suit their needs and budget. Some tour operators have holidays specifically for older age groups and, in recent years, the long-stay holiday has become popular with older people who can live relatively well and inexpensively through the winter months in resort hotels or other accommodation, in a warmer climate, even receiving their pensions while they are away.

Social Service Departments have the power to give financial help towards holidays. Having said this, some Authorities do not make grants at all, while others may offer holidays at places of their own choice instead of giving help. In addition, the amounts are never large and some use means-tests to determine the amount they will give.

GRANT-GIVING TRUSTS

A number of trusts give grants towards the costs of holidays, outings and treats. These are listed in *The Directory of Grant Making Trusts* which is published by The Charities Aid Foundation. Trusts and foundations vary tremendously in their policies and the way they respond to applications so it is important to try to learn as much as possible about a trust and its policy before applying. Details may be found in the directory, which is available at most libraries or from:

The Charities Aid Foundation
48 Pembury Road
Tonbridge
Kent TN9 2JD
Tel: 0732 771333

Listed below are names and addresses of some of these trusts:

The Abbey National Charitable Trust
Third Floor
Abbey House
201 Grafton Gate East
Milton Keynes, MK9 1AN

Alexandra Rose Day
1 Castelnau
Barnes
London SW13 9RP

The Dorothy Askew Trust
c/o Hodgson Harris
4 Kings Arms Yard
Moorgate
London EC2E 7AX

Assheton-Smith Charitable Trust
The Trustee Department
Coutts and Co
440 The Strand
London WC2R 0QS

The Charities Aid Foundation
48 Pembury Road
Tonbridge
Kent TN9 2JD

The Cotton Trusts
The Walled Garden
Tixover Grange
Nr Stamford
Lincs PE9 3QN

The Eeman Charitable Trust
18 Holly Mount
Hampstead
London NW3 6SG

Charles Henry Foyle Trust
c/o Boxfoldin Ltd
Merse Road
Redditch
Worcs B98 9HB

The Reader's Digest Trust
The Reader's Digest Association Ltd
25 Berkeley Square
London W1X 6AB
Tel: 071–629 8144

Further information on grant-giving trusts is available in Age Concern England's (address page 48) information sheet RS7. The leaflet also covers all other aspects of holidays for older and disabled people.

HOLIDAYS FOR PEOPLE WITH DISABILITIES

A number of organisations can assist with holidays for people with disabilities. These include:

Disabled Living Services
Redbank House
4 St Chad's Street
Cheetham
Manchester M8 8QA
Tel: 061–832 3678
Disabled Living Services organises group holidays and outings throughout the year for people with physical disabilities, their families and friends. Door-to-door transport is available if they live within the Greater Manchester area.

Greater London Association for Disabled People
336 Brixton Road
London SW9 7AA
Tel: 274 0107
Please send large sae for leaflet.

Holiday Services for Disabled Holidaymakers and Their Families
38 Brunswick Street
Teignmouth
Devon TQ14 8AF
Tel: 0626 779424
Please send sae for details of services and publications.

Other charities provide information on holidays and, in some cases, have their own holiday homes or organise holidays for special groups. Some of these holidays may be for members only. These charities include:

Arthritis Care
18 Stephenson Way
London NE1 2HD
Tel: 071–916 1500

The British Deaf Association
38 Victoria Place
Carlisle
Cumbria CA1 1HU
Tel: 0228 48844

The British Diabetic Association
10 Queen Anne Street
London W1M 0BD
Tel: 071–323 1531

The British Red Cross Society
9 Grosvenor Crescent
London SW1X 7EJ
Tel: 071–235 5454

The Disabled Drivers' Association
Holiday Hotel for Disabled People
Ashwellthorpe Hall Hotel
Ashwellthorpe
Norwich
Norfolk NR16 1EX
Tel: 050841 324

MIND
22 Harley Street
London W1N 2ED
Tel: 071–637 0741

Multiple Sclerosis Society
25 Effie Road
London SW6 1EE
Tel: 071–381 4022

Parkinson's Disease Society
22 Upper Woburn Place
London WC1H 0RA
Tel: 071–383 3513

Royal National Institute for the Blind
224 Great Portland Street
London W1N 6AA
Tel: 388 1266

The Winged Fellowship
Angel House
20–32 Pentonville Road
London N1 9XD
Tel: 071–833 2594
The Winged Fellowship is a charity which provides holidays and respite care for severely physically disabled people at five UK holiday centres and overseas. Disabled people come alone or with a carer. One-to-one care is provided by trained staff and volunteers and there is 24-hour nursing cover.

Special interest breaks range from riding to crafts or opera; outings are arranged each day to places of interest. A series of special weeks for Alzheimer's Disease sufferers and their carers is arranged each year. Phone for their 1994 brochure.

The Holiday Care Service
2 Old Bank Chambers
Station Road
Horley, Surrey RH6 9HW
Tel: 0293 774535
Helpline: 0891 515494
The charitable Holiday Care Service is the central resource for holiday information and support for people with disabilities, those on low incomes and those with other special needs. It provides information about holidays in the UK and abroad, and a booking service with discounted rates at UK accommodation. It also offers low-cost holidays under the 'Tourism for All' holidays scheme, and information on respite care.

The HCS's Holiday insurance policy is specifically designed for people with disabilities and their families. A selection of free information sheets are available (send a large sae), including:
Specialist Holidays for Disabled People
Accessible Hotels, Self-catering and Holiday Centre Accommodation in the UK
Transport Services for Disabled and Elderly People
Low-Cost Holidays
Activity and Special Interest Holidays
Financial Help for Holidays

Further Reading
A Guide for Disabled People, (The Royal Association of Disability and Rehabilitation, tel: 071–637 5400), £5 (inc p & p). Details more than 1000 specialised hotels, guest houses, self-catering properties, special centres and camp sites. It also lists voluntary and commercial organisations for people with disabilities, transport services and places to visit.

Age Concern England (address page 48) publishes a factsheet (No 4), *Holidays for Older People*, which aims to give suggestions on where to go and how to get information on holidays for older and disabled people. This includes information on locally organised holidays, financial help, commercial organisations, travelling abroad and holidays for people with disabilities and their carers.

Its factsheet on travel concessions (No 26), *Travel Information for Older People*, contains important information for older people.

TRAVELLING ABROAD

If an operator is chosen who is a member of The Association of British Travel Agents (ABTA), 55–57 Newman Street, London W1P 3PG, tel: 071–637 2444, the booking conditions will meet the ABTA Code of Conduct. Should the company fail financially the holiday or money will still be guaranteed. Any grievances should be taken up with the tour operator first. If this is not satisfactory, ABTA runs an arbitration scheme to deal with complaints.

Travel agent will be able to advise on whether any visas or special inoculations are needed. It is wise always to check in advance—people have been known to be refused entry into the country they wanted to visit.

Technically one is now not supposed to need a passport to travel to EC countries, but many transport carriers do ask for one and it is useful for identification purposes when cashing traveller's cheques or checking into a hotel.

LONG-STAY HOLIDAYS

These holidays have become very popular, offering reduced price accommodation in milder climes over the winter months.

All persons going for less than three months can cash all their retirement pension orders when they return. Remember that a pension order cannot be cashed later than three months after the date printed on it. If going abroad for three months or more, the local Social Security office should be warned well in advance to make arrangements for the payment of the pension, which can be paid into a bank in the UK for the duration.

If a person is receiving other Social Security benefits such as Housing Benefit and Income Support he or she should contact the local Social Security office before leaving the country.

Further Reading
Life in the Sun: A Guide to Long-stay Holidays and Living Abroad in Retirement, Nancy Tuft (Age Concern England, 1989), £6.95

HOLIDAY AND SPECIALIST ORGANISATIONS

Saga Holidays
The Saga Building
Middelburg Square
Folkestone
Kent CT20 1AZ
Tel: 0800 300500 (free) for UK, Europe
and Mediterranean holidays
0800 300400 (free) for cruises
0800 414383 (free) Travellers World,
America and Canada.
0800 414444 (free) Saga Flights Service
This is the largest provider of holidays
for people over 60 and offers a huge
range of holidays in the UK and overseas, including short breaks, cruises,
university and college centres, coach
holidays, touring centres, singles holidays, arts and special interest holidays,
holiday villages and holidays in practically every country in the world.

Countrywide Holidays
Birch Heys
Cromwell Range
Manchester M14 6HU
Tel: 061–225 1000
Countrywide holidays, which cele-
brated its centenary last year, offers a
wide variety of walking and special
interest holidays. Special interest holidays include visiting stately homes and
gardens, National Trust holidays,
bridge, dancing, coach tours, 'vintage'
holidays (for the over-60s), food and
drink, and natural history. Factsheets
and brochures for all holidays are
available on request.

The National Trust
36 Queen Anne's Gate
London SW1H 9AS
Tel: 071–222 9251

The National Trust for Scotland
5 Charlotte Square
Edinburgh EH2 4DU
Tel: 031–226 5922
The National Trust preserves historic
buildings, gardens, parks, countryside,
coastline and historic sites and also
offers holiday cottages in England,
Wales and Northern Ireland. It
publishes a free booklet, *Facilities for
Disabled and Visually Handicapped
Visitors*. The annual subscription
allows free entry into National Trust
properties.

Carefree Holidays Ltd
64 Florence Road
Northampton NN1 4NA
Tel: 0604 30382
Holidays for the over-55s in the UK
and overseas for the able and less able.

**Pre-retirement Association Holiday
Courses**
78 Capel Road
East Barnet
Herts EN4 8JF
Tel: 081–449 4506
Organises retirement planning holi-
days, in conjunction with Pontins
Holidays.

CRUSE—Bereavement Care
CRUSE House
126 Sheen Road
Richmond
Surrey TW9 1UR
Tel: 081–940 4818
Publishes *Holiday Ideas from CRUSE*
to help bereaved people when they are
on their own.

Travel Companions
110 High Mount
Station Road
London NW4 3ST
Tel: 081–202 8478
This organisation provides a nation-wide service for people aged 30–75 to share their holidays. People meet their travel companion before they decide to holiday together.

Major and Mrs Holt's Battlefield Tours
15 Market Street
Sandwich
Kent CT13 9DA
Tel: 0304 612248
This company arranges guided tours to First and Second World War and other battlefield areas and relatives' war graves in the UK and overseas.

Golden Rail Holidays
Ryedale Building
Piccadilly
York YO1 1NX
Tel: 0904 628992
Rail holidays

Shearings Ltd
Miry Lane
Wigan WN3 4AG
Tel: 0942 44246
Overseas and UK coach holidays

Chalfont Line Holidays
4 Medway Parade
Perivale
Middlesex UB6 8HA
Tel: 081–997 3799
Chalfont offers coach excursions and tailor-made breaks in the UK, as well as escorted air holidays to Switzerland, Holland, Malta or the Seychelles for disabled people.

RADAR (Royal Association for Disability and Rehabilitation)
25 Mortimer Street
London W1N 8AB
Tel: 071–637 5400
RADAR publishes holiday factsheets and books, including the *Annual Guide to Accommodation and Facilities Available in the UK* (£4.50) and *Holidays and Travel Abroad: Guide for Disabled People* (£3).

The British Deaf Association also arranges holidays—see page 35.

BREAK
20 Hooks Hill Road
Sheringham
Norfolk NR26 8NL
Tel: 0263 823170
BREAK provides respite care in a holiday environment for children and adults with learning disabilities or mental handicap. It also organises special breaks for single people over 40.

Intervac
International Home Exchange Service
3 Orchard Court
North Wraxall
Wilts SN14 7AD
Tel: 0225 892208
For an annual membership fee Intervac will put you in touch with thousands of families all over the world who wish to swap houses, thereby giving a rent-free holiday.

Co-op Holiday Care
PO Box 53
Corporation Street
Manchester M60 4ES
Tel: 061–832 7890
Arranges overseas, UK and long-stay holidays.

The British Trust for Conservation Volunteers
36 St Marys Street
Wallingford
Oxon OX10 0EL
For volunteers working on conservation projects.

Golden Years
Airtours plc
Holcombe Road
Helmshaw
Rossendale
Lancs BB4 4NB
Tel: 0706 830130 or 0706 240033
Short- and long-stay holidays in Europe.

Bakers Coaches
48 Locking Road
Weston-super-Mare
BS23 3DN
Tel: 0934 636636
Coach holidays.

Sun Island Holidays UK
Wroxall
Ventnor
Isle of Wight PO38 3BR
Tel: 0983 854532
Holidays in the Isle of Wight.

Scandinavian Seaways
Scandinavian House
Parkeston Quay
Harwich
Essex CO12 4QG
Tel: 0255 243456
Holidays and 'mini cruises' in Germany, Denmark and Scandinavia.

Leisurely Days
Enterprise (Owners Abroad)
Groundstar House
London Road, Crawley
W. Sussex RH10 2TB
Tel: 0293 560777
Long-stay holidays overseas.

The British Spas Federation
Central Information Services Unit
Thames Tower
Blacks Road
Hammersmith
London W6 9EL
Tel: 081–846 9000
Contact this branch of the British Tourist Authority for a listing of healthfarms and hydros.

The British Resorts Association
PO Box 9
Margate
Kent CT9 1XZ
Tel: 0843 225511
Advice on British resorts.

Great British Cities
2 Dolphin Square
London W4 2ST
Tel: 081–742 3388
City holidays.

H. F. Holidays
Imperial House
Edgware Road
London NW9 5AL
Tel: 081–905 9556
Activity holidays.

Grand UK Holidays
Aldwych House
Bethell Street
Norwich NR2 1NR
Tel: 0603 630 803
Holidays in the UK.

NADFAS Tours Ltd
Hermes House
80–89 Beckenham Road
Beckenham
Kent BR3 4RH
Tel: 081–658 2308
Art holidays.

Artscape
40–41 The Vintners
Temple Farm
Southend on Sea
Essex SS2 5RZ
Tel: 0702 601300
Art holidays.

ARP Over-50 Travel Club
Greencoat House
Francis Street
London SW1P 1DZ
Tel: 071–895 8880
The travel club of *050* magazine.

Care Home Holidays Ltd
Wern Manor
Portmadog
Gwynedd LL49 9SH
Tel: 0766 513322
Care home holidays.

National Express Coach Holidays
Victoria Station
London SW1
Tel: 071–7300202
Coach holidays.

Small and Friendly
Thomson Holidays
Greater London House
Hampstead Road
London NW3
Details available from travel agents.

David Urquhart Travel Ltd
103 Strathmore House
East Kilbride
G74 1LF
Coach holidays.

TRAVEL INSURANCE

It is advisable to take out insurance against the possible risks that may be encountered while on holiday. Household policies may cover loss or theft, but travellers should be sure to have coverage for medical and personal emergencies, which will cover cancellation and/or curtailment of the trip. Check that the cover required has been obtained, as most insurers impose terms or restrict cover for persons over 70.

The Holiday Care Service offers a holiday insurance policy specifically designed for people with disabilities and their families (see page 86.)

Travellers should be sure to check their household policy to find out what cover they have, as some policies can become invalid if the home is empty for more than two weeks. Housewatch is one of the agencies which will literally 'babysit' houses while their owners are away (see page 93)

Age Concern offers holiday travel insurance for people over 60:

Age Concern Insurance Services
Garrod House
Chaldon Road
Caterham
Surrey CR3 5YZ
Tel: 0883 346964

Other companies offering travel insurance for older people are:

Europ Assistance Ltd
Sussex House
Perrymount Road
Haywards Heath
W. Sussex RH16 1DN
Tel: 0444 440 202

Extrasure Holdings
Lloyd's Avenue House
6 Lloyds Avenue
London EC3N 3AX
Tel: 071–480 6871

Saga Insurance Services
The Saga Building
Middelburg Square
Folkestone
Kent CT20 1AZ

Alexander Stenhouse UK Ltd
65–71 London Road
Redhill
Surrey RH1 1YN
Tel: 0737 774177

A free leaflet about holiday and car insurance is available with sae from:

The Association of British Insurers
51 Gresham Street
London EC2V 7HQ
Tel: 071–600 3333

MEDICAL TREATMENT OVERSEAS

Medical treatment overseas may not be free nor of the same standard as in the UK. For emergency medical treatment in an EC country a person needs to have completed form E111 (available at post offices). It should then be stamped, signed and returned so that it may be taken along on the holiday. With the form is a useful leaflet, *Health Advice for Travellers Inside the European Community*.

In non-EC countries, emergency treatment may be provided on the same terms as for residents of the country being visited. Details of treatment available and charges are listed in leaflet T3, *Health Advice for Travellers Outside the European Community*, available from doctors' surgeries and Social Security offices.

For advice and information about health and safety guidelines and inoculations contact:

Travellers' Guides to Health
Health Publications Unit
No 2 Site
Heywood Stores
Manchester
Freephone: 0800 555777

HOME SECURITY WHILE AWAY

The security of one's home can be a nagging worry in the back of one's mind throughout a holiday. Housewatch can provide live-in security, including answering the telephone, caring for pets, watering plants, mowing the lawn and general housework. They can drive people to and from the airport and have some groceries awaiting their return.

Housewatch Ltd
Little London
Berdon
Bishop's Stortford
Herts CM23 1BE
Tel: 0279 777412

Homesitters Ltd
Buckland Wharf
Buckland
Aylesbury
Bucks HP22 5LQ
Tel: 0296 630730

Homewarmers
Old Pump House
Highwood
Ringwood
Hants BH24 3LZ
Tel: 0425 472898

Animal Aunts
Wydwooch
45 Fairview Road
Headley Down
Hants GU35 8HQ
Tel: 0428 712611
This company will look after pets in their owner's home.

TOURIST BOARDS

For general advice about travel in the British Isles, the appropriate tourist boards have many books, leaflets and brochures available, including advice for disabled people.

The English Tourist Board
Thames Tower
Blacks Road
Hammersmith
London W6 9EL
Tel: 081–846 9000

The Scottish Tourist Board
23 Ravelston Terrace
Edinburgh, EH4 3EU
Tel: 031–332 2433

The Irish Tourist Board (Bord Failte)
Ireland House
150 New Bond Street
London W2Y 0AQ
Tel: 071–493 3201

The Wales Tourist Board
Brunel House
2 Fitzalan Road
Cardiff CF2 1UY
Tel: 0222 499909

Northern Ireland Tourist Board
St Anne's Court
59 North Street
Belfast BT1 1NB
Tel: 0232 231221

State of Guernsey Tourist Board
PO Box 23
White Roack
St Peter Port
Guernsey, CI
Tel: 0481 726611

The national tourist office for other countries are mostly based in London. Telephone numbers are available from directory enquiries, the London telephone directory at the local library, or by contacting the relevant country's national airline.

chapter six

FINANCIAL MATTERS

Benefits, Investments and
How to Find Good Financial Advice

FINANCE IS A VAST SUBJECT. It affects us all, and often causes stress and concern, particularly among older people who may be concerned about not having sufficient money to live on, or that if they invest their 'nest egg' it will all be lost. Because of the apparent complexities and wide ranges of information available, it is often difficult to know where to find information or even to know what type of information one needs.

I have tried to keep this discussion of the subject as simple as possible. For the sake of clarity I have broken it into two broad categories: Benefits and Investments. First I examine the type of help and assistance that is available to those in need—including State pensions, war pensions, Income Support and Sick or Disability Benefit—and where to find it. In the latter half of this chapter I consider some of the range of options that are important to those who are more financially independent, including an explanation of the types of investment and savings that are available and indicating how to find a qualified and reputable adviser and what protection is available for the inexperienced investor.

All information is accurate at the time of writing; however, legislation is constantly changing the rates and types of benefit, and neither I nor the publishers can accept any responsibility for errors or omissions arising from advice taken from the book. It should not be treated as a complete and authoritative statement of the law. Readers must take due care in ensuring to the best of their ability that any course of action on which they embark is suitable for their requirements.

FINANCIAL ASSISTANCE AND BENEFITS

In this section I will consider the principal allowances and benefits that are available to the older person and to those in need of assistance (including the disabled and carers) who qualify for allowances and benefits; I also outline the organisations to contact for additional advice and help.

If limited provision or even no specific provision has been made for retirement, State Assistance is available to provide the basic necessities of life. The benefits available are essentially of two types:

1. Insured benefits, available by right if the requisite amount of National Insurance contributions have been paid. These include State Retirement Pension and State Earnings Related Pension.
2. Non-insured benefits, to which people may be entitled dependent upon their circumstances. Generally this involves means-testing. These include such benefits as Income Support.

Both of these categories are summarised below, together with a discussion of the help and benefits that are available for the sick and disabled, and those that care for them.

Some people feel that applying for assistance is akin to relying on charity. It is estimated that at least a million people over the age of 60 could receive extra help from the Government with their day-to-day expenses, housing costs or Council Tax but do not claim it. As the legislation is regularly changing and has done so particularly in the last few years, it is in everyone's interest to review carefully what is available to ensure that they are obtaining the maximum financial benefits available to them.

Many forms of benefit are complicated and have a wide variety of rules and exceptions attached to them. At the end of each section below I have listed books and leaflets that can be referred to, as well as the names of organisations that are able to give advice. The leaflets are free of charge and are available from all Social Security offices and most post offices and libraries. Anyone who is unable to find the leaflets locally should write (giving the leaflet titles and reference numbers to):

BA Publications
Heywood Stores
Manchester Road
Heywood
Lancs OL10 2PZ
or
Leaflets Unit
PO Box 21
Stanmore
Middlesex HA7 1AY

It is recommended that leaflets are obtained and, where necessary, contact the organisations mentioned for more advice.

There are also several free telephone numbers that can be called for more information about Social Security benefits and National Insurance.

- *Benefits Enquiry Line (BEL)*—0800 882 200. This is a confidential telephone service available for people with disabilities and their carers.
- *DSS Freeline* (general information on benefits)—0800 666555.
  This same information service about benefits is also available for other ethnic groups in the following languages:
      Chinese 0800 252451

Punjabi 0800 521360
Urdu 0800 289188
Welsh 0800 289011

The person you talk to will not, of course, have your (or your parent's) papers or all the details of your situation to hand. Therefore the advice provided must not be taken as a decision on any matter about which you are enquiring.

Information and explanations are also available from local Social Security offices (or the Benefits Agencies as they are often called, being executive agencies of the DSS) or Citizens Advice Bureaux. All can be found in the telephone book, listed under Social Security, Health & Social Security or Citizens Advice, or by asking at the local library. The address of the local office of the Citizens Advice Bureau can also be obtained by writing to the CAB's central office:

Citizens Advice Bureau—National Association
Myddleton House
115–123 Pentonville Road
London N1 9LZ
Tel: 071–833 2181

Scottish Association of Citizens Advice Bureau
82 Nicolson Road
Edinburgh EH8 9EW
Tel: 031–667 0156

NACAB S. Wales
Andrews Buildings
Suite 3–27, 67 Queen Street
Cardiff CF1 4AW
Tel: 0222 397686

NACAB N. Wales
134B High Street
Prestatyn
Clwyd LL19 9BN
Tel: 0745 856339

NACAB Northern Ireland Regional Office
11 Upper Crescent
Belfast BT7 1NT
Tel: 0232 231120

In addition, the local Age Concern group can provide services and advice. Their address can be found in the local telephone book or from the library, or by contacting the central offices of Age Concern:

Age Concern England
Astral House
1268 London Road
London SW16 4EJ
Tel: 081–679 8000

Age Concern Scotland
54a Fountainbridge
Edinburgh EH3 9PT
Tel: 031–228 5656

Age Concern Wales
1 Cathedral Road
Cardiff CF1 9SD
Tel: 0222 371821

Age Concern Northern Ireland
6 Lower Crescent
Belfast BT7 1NR
Tel: 0232 245729

Help the Aged can also provide help and advice:

Help the Aged
Information Department
St James's Walk
London EC1R 0BE
Tel: 071–253 0253
Help the Aged's Seniorline (Freephone 0800 289 404) offers advice on:

• welfare and disability benefits
• housing

• health
• support for carers
• mobility
• community alarms
• sources of local practical help
• other voluntary organisations.

Lines are open 10 a.m. to 4 p .m., Monday to Friday.

Additional Information
Disablement Information and Advice Line (DIAL): Look in the telephone book for the local number or telephone DIAL UK on 0302 310123.

Further Reading
Your Rights 1993–94, Sally West (published annually by Age Concern), £2.50
  This book is a guide to the State benefits available to older people, and contains advice on how to claim these benefits.
DSS leaflets:
  FB2 *Which Benefit—A Guide to Social Security and NHS Benefits*
  FB32 *Benefits after Retirement—What You Could Claim as a Pensioner*
Help the Aged also produces several useful leaflets:
  Can You Claim It? 1993
  A leaflet that deals with claiming benefits
  Claiming Disability Benefits
  A leaflet on benefits for sick and disabled people

State Retirement Pension (SRP)
The State Retirement Pension is a taxable weekly benefit payable to men when they reach 65 and women when they reach 60. It is possible to draw the pension even if work has not been given up completely, or alternatively it is possible to defer the pension for up to five years and thereby earn extra pension (or increments). If someone does continue to work after normal retirement age, it is no longer necessary for him or her to pay National Insurance (NI) contributions.

Payment of the SRP can be made direct to a nominated bank or building society every four or 13 weeks, or can be collected weekly from the post office. If your parent or relation is ill and/or is unable to collect the pension or any other benefit by going to the post office, he or she can sign on the back of each order or giro making it payable to a friend or relative. This person will be acting as an agent on your parent's behalf.

If your parent has more permanent difficulty in collecting the money, because for instance he or she has had a stroke or is mentally ill, the local Benefits Agency

(Social Security) office can arrange an *appointee* (who is normally a close friend or relative). If your parent is already being looked after by the Court of Protection (See Chapter 7 under Enduring Powers of Attorney) or has a legal representative, then those persons would become the appointee(s). Further details are available on DSS Form AP1 *A Helping Hand: How You Can Help Friends or Relatives Claim Social Security.*

The basic SRP is the same for men, for women who have paid their own NI contributions at the standard rate, and for widows. Married women who are not entitled to SRP on the basis of their own contributions may get one on the basis of their husband's contributions, but only when he is already receiving a pension and the woman is over 60.

The basic rate is currently (1993) £56.10 a week for a single person and £89.80 for a married couple.

To receive a full-rate Basic Pension, persons must have 'qualifying years' for about 90 per cent of their working lives. A qualifying year is a tax year in which a person receives qualifying earnings (on which standard rate Class 1 NHI contributions have been paid) of at least 52 times the lower earnings limit for that year. If your parent is concerned that there may be gaps in his or her NI payment record, you can ask the local Benefits Agency (Social Security) office for advice.

SRP is not paid automatically. It must be claimed. This can be done up to four months before retirement using Form BR 1, which should be sent to the retiring person automatically. If one is not received by three months before retirement, the local Benefits Agency (Social Security) office should be approached.

If standard rate NI contributions have been paid by someone as an employee after 4 April 1978 it may be possible to claim an *additional earnings related pension.* If NI contributions were paid as an employee between 1961 and 1975 it may also be possible to claim a *Graduated Pension.*

If an individual is over 80, supports another adult or has children (for whom he or she is entitled to claim Child Benefit), it may be possible to claim an *additional weekly payment.* Also, anyone receiving Invalidity Allowance with an Invalidity Benefit within eight weeks of reaching pensionable age may be entitled to an additional Invalidity Payment.

Further Reading
The DSS provide further information in the following leaflets:
FB6 *Retiring?*
FB32 *Benefits after Retirement*
Both provide general information on the range of benefits and services for people in retirement (FB32 is to supersede FB6 eventually).
DSS leaflet NP45 *A Guide to Widow's Benefits*
DSS leaflet NP46 *A Guide to Retirement Pensions*
Leaflet NP46 provides details of all aspects of retirement pensions.
DSS leaflet NI92 *Giving up Your Retirement Pension to Earn Extra*
DSS leaflet NI184 *Over 80s pensions*

Special Circumstances

People Who Have Been Divorced

If your parent is divorced and is not entitled to a full Basic Pension, his or her former spouse's NI record may be taken into account if it will provide a better pension, providing that your parent has not remarried before pensionable age. It is not necessary to wait until the former spouse is receiving his or her pension. For further information see DSS leaflet NP46, *A Guide to Retirement Pensions*, and NI95, *National Insurance for Divorced Women*.

People Going into Hospital

If your parent needs to go into hospital for in-patient treatment on the NHS, the pension will be reduced after six weeks. For further information see DSS leaflet NI9, *Going into Hospital*.

People Going Abroad

Your parent can normally get his or her pension paid anywhere abroad. If the trip is for less than three months and your parent is receiving orders or giros which are normally cashed at the post office, it is possible to let them accumulate and cash them all at once. However, orders over three months old may not be cashed.

If your parent is going for between three and six months, it is possible to have the pension paid into a bank account. If he or she is going for more than six months, the pension can be paid to him or her abroad.

If your parent or parents are living abroad when the pension rates go up in the UK, they will receive the increased rate if they are living in a European Community (EC) country or in a non-EC country with which the UK has a reciprocal arrangement. If they are living in a non-EC country with no such arrangement, the pension will remain the same as when they left the country.

For further details see:

DSS leaflet NI38 *Social Security Abroad*

DSS leaflet NI106 *Pensioners or Widows Going Abroad*

Alternatively, you can write to:

DSS Benefits Agency
Overseas Directorate
Newcastle upon Tyne NE98 1YX

War Pensions Schemes

Anyone who has been disabled as a result of service in HM Armed Forces between 1914 and 1921 or at any time after September 1939 (and in certain cases any civilians disabled as a result of the Second World War, and merchant seamen disabled due to war) is entitled to a War Disablement Pension. Any widow, widower or dependent relative of someone who has died as a result of such an injury or disability is entitled to a War Widow's Pension (see below).

Pensions for disability or death caused by service in HM Armed Forces between 1 October 1921 and 2 September 1939 are the responsibility of the Ministry of Defence. For more information, write to the relevant address below:

Army
MoD
Army Pensions Office
Kentigern House
65 Brown Street
Glasgow G2 8EX

Royal Navy and Marines
MoD
NPP (Acs) 3A
HMS Centurion
Grange Road
Gosport PO13 9XA

Royal Air Force
MoD
F2 (Air Gloucester)
Building 56
RAF Innsworth
Gloucester GL3 1HW

War Pensions are not taxable. Claims for War Pensions should be made in writing to:

War Pensions Directorate
Benefits Agency
North Fylde Central Office
Norcross
Blackpool FY5 3TA

There is also a War Pensions Helpline on 0253 858858.

The War Pensions Schemes are separate from the Social Security Schemes. Therefore persons claiming War Pensions may also be able to claim other allowances, such as Attendance Allowance. Details are available from the local Benefits Agency (Social Security) office.

Further details are also available in leaflets MPL 153, *Guide for the War Disabled*, and MPL154, *Rates of War Pensions and Allowances*.

It is possible for a person to claim War Pensions even if living abroad. Details are available on leaflet MPL120, *War Pensioners and War Widows Going Abroad*. Further advice and assistance are also available from the War Pensions Directorate (for address and Helpline, see above).

War Disablement Pension (WDP)
Individuals may receive a WDP if their disability was a result of, or was made worse by, service in HM Armed forces between 1914 and 1921 or at any time since 1939.

There are no time limits for claiming. Payment can, however, be made only from the date of the claim. The amount paid depends upon the severity of the disability and the rank of the person claiming.

People who are less than 20 per cent disabled will receive a lump sum instead of a pension. Since January 1993, deafness which causes less than a 20 per cent disability is excluded from the conditions that count towards a War Pension.

WDP is from £19.44 per week for 20 per cent disability to £97.20 per week for 100 per cent disability. WDP is paid tax-free and in addition to most Social Security benefits.

War Widow's or Dependant's Pension

A pension is also available for the widows, widowers, orphan children and close relatives of someone killed in the Armed Forces or who subsequently died of an injury sustained while in the Armed Forces.

A War Widow's Pension is payable on the death of war pensioners who were receiving constant Attendance Allowance. The amount of the pension is determined by a means-test, the rank of the person who has died and the age of the widow.

It is not possible for someone to claim a War Widow's Pension as well as a National Insurance Widow's Pension. It is, however, possible to claim the benefits and allowances which have been earned by the deceased person's own contributions.

Further details are available in leaflet MPL152, *War Widows and Other Dependents.*

War Pensioner's Welfare Service (WPWS)

Additional assistance may also be available from the WPWS, which advises and assists war pensioners on pension matters or any other problems. The service works closely with local authority social services and other voluntary organisations that help disabled ex-servicemen and their families. The address of the nearest WPWS office is available from the local Benefits Agency (Social Security) office or from the back of leaflet MPL153, *Guide for the War Disabled.*

Useful Addresses

Occupational Pensions Advisory Service (OPAS)
11 Belgrave Road
London SW1V 1RP
Tel: 071–233 8080
OPAS is an independent voluntary organisation giving free help and advice to members of the public concerned about their pension rights on all matters about personal or company pension schemes. The OPAS service is available to anyone who believes that he or she has pension rights, including working members of pension schemes, pensioners, those with deferred pensions from previous employment, and dependents.

Royal British Legion
48 Pall Mall
London SW1Y 5JY
Tel: 071–973 0633

The Royal British Legion will help
most ex-service people with claims or
appeals for War Pensions.

Income Support (IS)

Income Support is a Social Security benefit available to assist people whose total
family income falls below a certain level: It can be paid on top of other benefits
including State Retirement Pension, and does not depend upon NI contributions
that have been paid.

People over 60 are eligible if they:
a) reside in Great Britain
b) do not work nor have a partner working more than 16 hours a week
c) do not have combined capital with their partner of in excess of £8,000.
   Savings between £3,000 and £8,000 will affect the amount available. Each
   £250 of savings in excess of £3,000 is treated as income of £1 per week.

To determine if one is eligible for IS, two figures must be calculated: how much
the Government thinks you need each week to manage on (the 'applicable
amount') and the amount of net weekly income you have. The computation of
net weekly income is complicated. Any savings are converted to weekly income.
For married persons, or people living together as though they are married, the
income and savings of both parties are added together.

As an example, the 'applicable amount' for a single person aged 65 living alone
is £61.30 per week. This increases to £67.55 if they are 80 or over or to £101.25
if they are severely disabled.

The amount of IS that anyone is entitled to consists of three main components:
1. a prescribed personal allowance for each person, which covers payments
   towards day-to-day living expenses
2. a premium for groups of people with special needs, such as people with
   disabilities, people over 60, people who are receiving Invalid Care
   Allowance and those with dependent children. These premiums are addi-
   tions to the personal allowances
3. an allowance to cover housing costs, such as mortgage interest or other costs
   not met by Housing Benefit.

Many people claim IS only to find that they are awarded a small amount each
week. They therefore think that the bother of claiming is not worth while.
However, apart from it being that person's right to claim, perhaps more impor-
tantly it is a passport to other types of help. For instance, if someone is eligible
for IS, he or she will also have their Council Tax paid and, probably, the rent or
any interest on a mortgage or home loan. (For further information, see the section
on Council Tax Benefit and Housing Benefit, below).

In addition, he or she will obtain free NHS prescriptions, dental treatment, eye
tests and vouchers to help with the cost of glasses, and assistance with the cost
of travelling to hospital for NHS treatment. If that person lives in a private or
voluntary nursing or residential care home where fees must be met from private

means, he or she can receive IS to assist with the fees. There are special and quite complicated rules for working out how much is available. The local Benefits Agency (Social Security) office will be able to provide more information. Information is also available in DSS leaflet IS50, *Help for People Who Live in Residential Care Homes or Nursing Homes*. See also Counsel and Care's factsheet No 6 (details below).

Further Information
DSS leaflet IS1 *Income Support—See If You Are Entitled*
DSS leaflet IS20 *A Guide to Income Support*
DSS leaflet AB11 *Help with NHS Costs*
C & C factsheet No 14 *Income Support for Older People at Home*
C & C factsheet No 6 *Claiming Income Support towards the Fees of a Registered Private or Voluntary Home*
Factsheets 14 and 6 are produced by:

Counsel and Care
Lower Ground Floor
Twyman House
16 Bonny Street
London NW1 9PG

For Sick, Injured or Disabled People
There are a wide range of benefits for people who are sick, injured or disabled. For general information about the benefits available, refer to DSS leaflet F28, *Sick or disabled?*

Invalidity Benefit
This benefit is tax-free and comprises several separate components.

Invalidity Pension is usually paid to people before retirement who are incapable of working for more than 28 weeks, (after 28 weeks off work normal Statutory Sick Pay or Sickness Benefits end). Eligibility for Invalidity Pension is dependent upon enough full National Insurance contributions having been paid. An extra payment may be claimed if the claimant worked after April 1978, or if he or she first became incapable of work before 60 (men) or 55 (women). Invalidity Pension and the extra payments are together known as Invalidity Benefit.

When a person reaches retirement age, it is possible to choose between Invalidity Benefit and the State Retirement Pension. Although the difference between the two might be small, it is important to remember that Invalidity Benefit is tax-free, whereas Retirement Pension is taxable. No one may stay on Invalidity Benefit for more than five years after pensionable age.

It is often difficult to decide whether it is better to remain on Invalidity Benefit or change to Retirement Pension. It is necessary to check whether other benefits such as Income Support, Council Tax Benefit or Housing Benefit would be affected by the change. It is advisable to speak to one of the independent bodies, such as the local Citizens Advice Bureau, Age Concern or Help the Aged.

Further information is available from DSS leaflet NI16A, *Invalidity Benefit*.

Severe Disablement Allowance (SDA)

Severe Disablement Allowance is a tax-free benefit, normally payable to persons of working age who have been unable to work for at least 28 weeks due to long-term sickness or severe mental or physical disability. SDA is normally paid to those who have not paid enough National Insurance contributions to receive Sickness or Invalidity Benefit.

To qualify for SDA a person must have a severe disability (at least 80 per cent disabled) and be under 65 when SDA is first claimed. Once claimed it can be paid to any age.

SDA is £33.70 per week (1993), but an age-related supplement is paid on top. Some married women may not be getting the correct amount of age-related supplement; all should receive at least £3.75 per week. Also some women who in the past received Non-Contributory Invalidity Pension and then transferred to Retirement Pension may be due an age-related supplement now.

If a person is claiming Income Support, it will be reduced by the amount of SDA received. However, as there may be long-term advantages in claiming, I would recommend that it is always worth making a claim.

If anyone thinks they may be entitled to an age-related supplement, they should refer to their local Benefits Agency (Social Security) office or Citizens Advice Bureau.

For further information see DSS leaflet NI252, *Severe Disablement Allowance*.

Attendance Allowance (AA)

Attendance Allowance is a tax-free weekly cash benefit for disabled people over 65 who require a lot of personal care (such requirement starting after they are 65) because of their physical or mental disability. Anyone who had care needs before their 65th birthday should claim Disability Living Allowance (see below).

AA is not means-tested, does not depend upon National Insurance contributions made and can be paid in addition to other benefits, including Income Support.

Two rates are available—a lower one of £30 per week for people who are so severely physically or mentally disabled that they require looking after by day or by night, but not for both, and a higher one of £44.90 for people with similar disability who need looking after both day and night or for those who are not expected to live for more than six months and who need looking after both day and night.

For further information see DSS leaflet DS702, *Attendance Allowance*. The leaflet includes a reply slip to send for a claim pack. If your parent is in a position to claim, it should be sent off as soon as possible, as the date the DSS receives the slip will normally be the date from which the benefit is calculated. The claim form is very lengthy, but normally a medical examination is not necessary.

Further Information
Factsheet 11 *Attendance Allowance for People aged 65 and Over*
 Produced by:

Counsel and Care
Lower Ground Floor
Twyman House
16 Bonny Street
London NW1 9PG

Constant Attendance Allowance (CAA)
Constant Attendance Allowance is an extra allowance paid on top of War Disability Pensions or pensions for disability or illness caused by accident or disease at work. It is paid to people who need daily care and attention, and whose disability has been assessed at 100 per cent. There are four rates; how much is paid depends on how much attention is needed.

CAA and Attendance Allowance may not be claimed at the same time.

For people who are at the top or intermediate rate of CAA, there is also an additional allowance called Exceptionally Severe Disablement Allowance. This is paid to people who need constant care and attention. There is no need to claim for it, as each person claiming CAA is automatically considered.

For more information see the following leaflets:
NI2 *If You Have an Industrial Disease*
NI6 *Industrial Injuries Disablement Benefit*

Disability Living Allowance (DLA)
Disability Living Allowance is a tax-free benefit for people under 65 who need help with personal care or with getting around because of illness or disability. People disabled after they reach the age of 65 are not eligible for DLA and should claim Attendance Allowance. People aged between 65 and 66 may still claim if they started to need help before their 65th birthday.

DLA is not affected by any savings or (usually) income that the person claiming or his or her partner might have. It does not depend upon National Insurance contributions made and it may be paid in addition to other benefits, including Income Support.

DLA may still be paid even if no one is providing the care the individual needs. However, normally the person must have needed help for at least three months and be likely to need it for at least a further six months. Persons who are not expected to live for longer than six months have no need to wait for the initial three-month period.

There are two components of DLA:
1. help with personal care, and
2. help with mobility.
The personal care component is paid at one of three rates. The higher rate (£44.90 per week) is for those not expected to live for more than six months, or for those

who are so disabled that they require help from another person both day and night. The middle rate (£30 per week) is for those who need help from another person either during the day or during the night. The lower rate (£11.95 per week) is for those who require help for a significant portion of the day (generally about one hour) whether at one time or over a number of periods.

The mobility component is similar to the old Mobility Allowance and is paid at one of two rates. The higher rate is for those who have such severe physical or mental disability that they are unable or virtually unable to walk, or who are deaf or blind or require someone to look after them on a constant basis in order to protect both themselves and others. The lower rate is for those who can walk but are so severely physically or mentally disabled that they are unable to take advantage of being out of doors without guidance or supervision from another person most of the time.

Leaflet DS704 (see below) includes a reply slip to send for a claim pack. This should be sent off as soon as possible, as the date the DSS receives the slip will normally be the date from which the benefit is calculated. The claim form is very lengthy, but normally no medical examination is necessary. Any claim should be dealt with within six weeks; if there are delays or any hardship is suffered as a result of a delay, a complaint should be registered with the Customer Service Manager at the Disability Living Centre where the claim is being dealt with. If the claim is turned down or is awarded on a lower scale than expected, it is possible to appeal against the decision.

For further information see the following DSS leaflets:

DS704 *Disability Living Allowance.*

HB6 *Equipment and Services for Disabled People*

HB6 is also available in Bengali, Chinese, Greek, Gujarati, Hindi, Punjabi, Turkish, Urdu, Vietnamese and Welsh.

Help the Aged—*Claiming Disability Benefits*

For those living in Scotland, the Scottish Home and Health Department provides a leaflet entitled *Help for the Handicapped in Scotland.*

Further Reading
The Way Around Disability Living Allowance and Disability Working Allowance: A Critical Guide. Available from:

Disability Alliance
Universal House
88–94 Wentworth Street
London E1 7SA
price £3.50, including p & p
The Disability Rights Handbook (Disability Alliance), £7.95 including p & p; £5 to people on any means-tested benefit

Help for Carers

In addition to the benefits and allowances paid to those who are sick and disabled, there are a number of benefits that are available to carers. These benefits do not distinguish whether the person being cared for is a friend or a relative, whether you provide care on your own or jointly and whether it is for a few hours a week or full time.

Invalid Care Allowance (ICA)

ICA is a taxable weekly cash allowance which can be claimed by people of working age who are caring for a severely disabled person. The person being cared for must be receiving one of these three: Disability Allowance (at either the higher or middle rate for help with personal care), Attendance Allowance (at either of the two rates) or Constant Attendance Allowance (paid at more than the half-day rate under the Industrial Injuries *or* War Pensions scheme).

ICA is not means-tested and does not depend upon National Insurance contributions paid. It is, however, dependent upon the carer earning less than £50 per week after allowable expenses and spending at least 35 hours per week as a carer.

The basic rate of ICA is £33.70 a week. If the carer has other people to support, such as children or a spouse, he or she may receive more than the basic rate. If the carer is receiving Income Support, Housing Benefit or Council Tax Benefit, he or she will be entitled to a special Carer's Premium. It is as well to ask for advice in this situation, particularly with Income Support, as the rules become quite complex. For example, if a carer is receiving Income Support when he or she starts to receive ICA, the ICA will be taken off the Income Support; however, as a result of Carer Premium being added on, the carer will be better off.

ICA is a taxable benefit. It should be claimed before the age of 65. Although it can continue to be paid after the age of 65 it cannot be paid on top of the State Retirement Pension; it is possible to claim the higher of the two.

ICA may be claimed, subject to certain conditions, irrespective of whether the carer is related to or living at the same address of the person being cared for.

To claim, a claim pack DS700 should be obtained from the local Benefits Agency (Social Security) office or Citizens Advice Bureau.

For further information see DSS leaflet FB31, *Caring for Someone*.

Home Responsibilities Protection (HRP)

HRP is a scheme to make sure that people do not receive less State Pension because, during their working life, they have taken time away from work to look after someone who is sick or disabled.

The rules for getting HRP are:

- the carer must be regularly engaged for at least 35 hours a week in caring for someone who receives one of these three benefits: the Disability Living Allowance care component (at the highest or middle rate), Attendance Allowance or Constant Attendance Allowance for a minimum of 48 weeks in the year, or
- the carer must be receiving Income Support, and not be required to be avail-

able for employment because of the care duties at home.

If the carer receives Income Support he or she will receive HRP automatically. If the person being cared for receives Attendance Allowance or Constant Attendance Allowance, the carer needs to apply for HRP.

For more information, see the notes that come with form NP27, *Application Form for Home Responsibilities Protection*, and NP46, *A Guide to Retirement Pensions*.

Council Tax Benefit (CTB)

Anyone receiving Income Support does not have to pay Council Tax. It is also still possible to get help with Council Tax even if your income or capital is considered too high for you to get Income Support. The help is called Council Tax Benefit, and is worked out in a similar way to Income Support.

Many people who did not receive help with their community charge will nevertheless be eligible for CTB, although in certain cases the reverse is also true. If someone received Community Charge Benefit, the council should work out any entitlement to CTB. The amount of help individuals are entitled to depends upon the amount of money that they or their partner have coming in, the size of their family, their combined savings, the amount of Council Tax to be paid and whether other dependents share the same home.

To determine if someone is eligible for CTB it is necessary to work out three figures:

1. The applicable amount, as specified for Income Support (see page 103)
2. Net weekly income, in the same way as for Income Support
3. Net weekly Council Tax. This is calculated by dividing the Council Tax payable on the property (after allowing for reductions because of the number and type of people living in the property and possible transition relief because the Council Tax is much more than the community charge) by 365 and then multiplying by 7.

The Council Tax Benefit available is then calculated by:

• taking the applicable amount away from the net income
• dividing the result by 5
• taking the result away from the net weekly Council Tax.

If the answer is more than zero, that should be the amount of the CTB. If the answer is less than zero, then no CTB is payable.

If your parent is on Income Support, CTB can be claimed at the same time. A form to claim CTB is included with the IS claim form. The office dealing with your parent's claim will pass the form directly to the council. If your parent is not on Income Support but you believe that he or she might be eligible for CTB, contact the local borough or district council office.

For further information, refer to DSS leaflet CTB1, *Help with the Council Tax*. This leaflet is also available in Welsh.

A similar leaflet (referred to as CTB2) is also available in the following languages: Arabic, Bengali, Chinese, Greek, Gujerati, Hindi, Punjabi, Somali, Turkish, Urdu, Vietnamese.

Second Adult Rebate

This is a special Council Tax Benefit which can be paid in some cases even if an individual's income or savings are too high to get normal CTB, although it is not possible to claim both at the same time. It is called Second Adult Rebate and can be claimed by someone who is single but has another person living in his or her home who meets specific conditions. This other person must be:

• aged 18 or older
• not paying rent
• not living as though married with the claimant
• not paying Council Tax him- or herself
• on a low income.

If the person living in the house is on Income Support, it is possible to claim a rebate of 25 per cent of the Council Tax. If his or her gross income is £105 or less, it is possible to get a rebate of 15 per cent of the Council Tax.

If you wish to find out more or believe that your parent is eligible, you should contact the local council.

Housing Benefit

In the same way that people are eligible for Council Tax Benefit, so certain people who are tenants may receive help with their rent. This help is called Housing Benefit and is calculated in a similar way to Council Tax Benefit, except that net weekly rent is used instead of net weekly Council Tax.

The benefit is calculated in a complicated manner, but can be summarised as follows:

• take the applicable amount away from the net income
• multiply the result by 0.65
• take that result away from the net weekly rent.

If the answer is 50p or more, then that is the approximate amount of Housing Benefit you would receive per week to help pay the rent. If the answer is less than zero then no Housing Benefit is available.

If your parent is on Income Support, Housing Benefit may be claimed at the same time, as with Council Tax Benefit. The Benefits Agency (Social Security) office will pass the information to your parent's local council. If your parent is not on Income Support but you believe that he or she might be in a position to claim Housing Benefit, your parent should go to the local council for assistance.

Housing Benefit is awarded for limited periods which are set by the council. A fresh claim must be made at the end of each period.

For further information see RR1 Housing Benefit: *Help with Your Rent*—available from council offices; RR2 *A Guide to Housing Benefit and Council Tax Benefit*—available from a Social Security office.

Local Services

If your parent is disabled he or she might benefit from the special range of services provided by the local authority's Social Services Department. For instance, the Social Services Department may help with:

- bus and train fares
- special equipment and aids or adaptations to the home
- home helps
- day centres
- residential accommodation
- laundry
- holidays
- meals on wheels
- provision of telephone and television
- advice from a social worker.

For further information see Chapter 3 of this book or ask at your local Citizens Advice Centre or your local council's Social Services Department.

Also available from the local Benefits Agency (Social Security) office is the *Door to Door Guide* for information about transport for disabled people, published by the Department of Transport. British Rail also produces a leaflet available from all stations and entitled, *The Railcard for Disabled People.* See also Chapter 10 of this book.

Some local transport services offer free or reduced price travel on buses or the London Underground. In addition, anyone over 60 can buy a British Rail Senior Citizens Railcard allowing the holder to buy some tickets at a reduced price. Enquire from British Rail Information Offices, London Regional Transport or your local bus service company. For further information, see Chapter 10 (page 167).

Free NHS Prescriptions

All persons over retirement age automatically get free NHS prescriptions. Any person (or his or her partner) on Family Credit or Income Support receives free NHS dental treatment, wigs and fabric supports, prescriptions and vouchers for glasses. For further information see Chapter 2 of this book.

War and service pensioners may get additional assistance with glasses and dental treatment, and may receive assistance with other NHS charges for their pensioned disability.

The Department of Health provides the following leaflets:

AB11 *Help with NHS Costs*
D11 *NHS Dental Treatment*
H11 *NHS Hospital Travel Costs*
P11 *NHS Prescriptions*
G11 *NHS Sight Tests and Vouchers for Glasses*
WF11 *NHS Wigs and Fabric Supports*

These leaflets are available at any GP's surgery; AB11 is available from some post offices; all are also available from:

The Health Publications Unit

No 2 Site
Heywood Stores
Manchester Road
Heywood
Lancs L10 2PZ

Help the Aged provides free leaflets called *Health Benefits* and *Going into Hospital*. Both leaflets provide additional information on what assistance might be available.

Additional information is provided in Chapter 2 of this book.

The Social Fund

The Social Fund was created to help people to be able to meet exceptional expenses that they could not provide out of regular income. There are two kinds of benefit: grants that are available by right (if the law says that a payment should be made, anyone who is eligible will receive it) in certain prescribed circumstances, and also interest-free loans and Community Care grants that are discretionary rather than paid by right. Grants and payments do not usually have to be repaid.

The right to help from the Social Fund does not depend upon National Insurance contributions having been paid, but means-testing is used.

Payments by Right

These payments are grants and do not have to be repaid. They cover three areas:
1. cold weather payments
2. funeral payments
3. maternity payments.
I will only discuss the first two here, as the third is not likely to be relevant.

Cold Weather Payments

Cold Weather Payments of £6 per week are paid to persons receiving Income Support that includes one of the following premiums:
• a pension because the person or his or her partner is over 60
• a disability premium
• a disabled child premium because his or her child is getting either
Attendance Allowance or Mobility Allowance or is registered as blind.
The payments are made whenever the forecast for the local area shows that the temperature is likely to be 0°C or below for a period of seven days or more. The payments are automatically sent to each eligible person, so no claim has to be made. If, however, no payment is received within one month of the announcement of the cold weather, contact the local Benefits Agency (Social Security) office.

For further information see leaflet CWP1 *Extra Help with Heating Costs When It's Very Cold*.

Age Concern also produces a leaflet called *Help with Heating*.

Funeral Payments

Funeral Payments are limited to people with specified low-income benefits such as Income Support. Each benefit is to assist towards the cost of a simple funeral. Claims for a funeral must be made within three months after the date of the funeral. The benefits are reduced if the savings of the person or partner of the person claiming are in excess of £500 for people aged under 60 and £1000 for people aged 60 and over.

For further information see DSS leaflet D49 *What to Do after a Death* (Funeral Payments).

Discretionary Payments

Discretionary payments from the Social Fund are determined by local Benefits Agencies (Social Security) offices. There is no legal framework of entitlements; decisions about payments are taken by Social Fund officers acting under the directions and guidance issued by the Secretary of State. As a limited amount of money is made available by the Government, each DSS office is provided with a fixed amount which they have to distribute accordingly. If, for instance, they pay all the available money out in the first six months of the year, all subsequent applications, regardless of their severity, may have to be turned down.

There are three types of payment:
1. Community Care Grants
2. Budgeting Loans
3. Crisis Loans.

Community Care Grants

These grants are intended to help certain groups of people who are facing special difficulty or hardship to lead independent lives in the community. Primarily they are aimed to assist individuals and families such as the elderly, handicapped, chronically ill or disabled. For further information, see chapters 3 and 4 of this book.

Grants may be awarded to help those establishing themselves in the community after they have come out of hospital, care or other institution. They may also be awarded to keep people within the community living in their own homes. In certain cases the grants may be awarded to ease exceptional pressures on families as a result of long-term illness or family breakdown.

The grants may cover the cost of a variety of household items such as furniture, bedding and clothes. In certain circumstances they may also cover removal costs, minor house repairs or travelling expenses—to attend a relative's funeral for instance, or visit someone who is ill. Grants are not available for expenses that the local authority has a statutory duty to meet.

Community Care Grants are only available to people on Income Support or to those who expect to be on Income Support when they move into the community. If the person to receive the grant, or that person and his or her partner, has savings of over £1,000 (£500 for those under 60), the grant will be reduced by the extra amount of the savings.

The Community Care Grant is not a loan and does not have to be repaid.

To apply for a Community Care Grant, your parent should ask the local Benefits Agency (Social Security) office for Form SF300.

Budgeting Loans

Budgeting Loans are interest-free loans that are available to people who have been receiving Income Support for at least 26 weeks. They are available to help spread large one-off costs over a longer period.

A loan might be made to allow the recipient to purchase essential household furniture, such as a cooker or bed, or to pay for essential repairs or removal expenses. Loans are not available for fuel bills or general housing costs (although certain exceptions are made when intermittent costs are not met by Housing Benefit or Income Support).

The minimum loan is £30 and the maximum that may be outstanding at any one time is £1,000. If the applicant for the loan (together with his or her partner) has savings of over £1000 (£500 for those under 60) the loan will be reduced by the excess.

A Budgeting Loan is interest-free and repayable. The Social Fund Officer who approves the loan must ensure that the person receiving it can afford to repay it, usually by weekly deductions from the Income Support for up to 18 months. The rate of deduction (normally between 5 per cent and 15 per cent per week) is based upon an individual's income and general circumstances. If Income Support is stopped, the loan becomes immediately repayable.

Two important pieces of advice need to be heeded before applying for a Budgeting Loan:
1. Apply for a Community Care Grant rather than a Budgeting Loan.
2. If a Community Care Grant is not given for the item or service needed, seek advice from the local Citizens Advice Bureau before applying for a Budgeting Loan.

Crisis Loans

Crisis Loans are to help people with immediate short-term expenses that have arisen as the result of an emergency or a disaster. They may only be claimed if there is no other way of preventing serious risk or damage to the health or safety of your family. To claim the loan it is *not* necessary to be on Income Support or to receive any other form of benefit, although any money that the person may have is taken into account when the claim is assessed.

Loans have been given, for instance, in circumstances where people have lost their money, lost their belongings in a fire or have been stranded away from home.

The loans can cover both living expenses (usually for up to 14 days) or something that is needed urgently such as household equipment or travel costs. Loans are not available for such things as holidays, mobility needs, televisions, telephones or motor vehicle costs (except for emergency travelling expenses).

The loan is interest-free but repayable, either by weekly deductions from benefit or in some other way. The rate and period of repayment are based upon available income and other general circumstances.

To apply for a Crisis Loan, your parent should contact the local Benefits Agency (Social Security) office, or the nearest one if he or she is away from home.

For further information on the Social Fund, see the following DSS leaflets:

SFL2 *How the Social Fund Can Help You*

SB16 *A Guide to the Social Fund*

Counsel and Care produce a leaflet called *The Social Fund for Older People.* Their address is on page 49 of this chapter.

Reviews and Appeals

If someone has applied for a Community Care Grant, Budgeting Loan or a Crisis Loan and is not happy with the decision he or she can apply for a review by writing to the local Benefits Agency (Social Security) office within 28 days of the decision. It is important to give clear reasons why it is considered that a review is necessary. It is not possible to ask for a review on the size of instalments that have to be paid, although if circumstances change this can then be reconsidered.

If a satisfactory reply is not received to the review, it is possible to ask the Social Fund Inspector to look at your application. The Inspector is independent of the DSS. The local Benefits Agency (Social Security) office should be contacted if you wish to apply to the Inspector.

If someone has applied for a Funeral Payment and is not happy with the decision, it is possible to appeal. Also if a person thinks he or she should have had a Cold Weather Payment, he or she can appeal. To appeal, it is necessary to write to the local Benefit Agency (Social Security) office within three months of the decision, giving reasons why an appeal is justified.

Further information on reviews and appeals:

Leaflet NI246 *How to Appeal*

Leaflet NI260 *A Guide to Reviews and Appeals*

Money Advice and How to Deal with Problems

Anyone who is on Income Support can obtain free advice on how to manage money. This advice could be of help to those who often find themselves in financial difficulty. A discussion can be arranged at home or in the local Benefits Agency (Social Security) office. The objective will be to find a way to balance income and outgoings. If required, assistance can also be given in negotiating on the person's behalf with people to whom he or she owes money.

For further assistance or for those in debt, refer to Chapter 7 (the section headed 'Debt'). In it is an explanation of what can be done if someone is in severe financial difficulty. Two organisations, National Debtline and Money Management Council, are available to help. Their addresses and telephone numbers are provided (see page 145).

Further information is provided in *Thinking about Money*, a free booklet published by Help the Aged in association with the Birmingham Settlement. It aims to show a person how to assess the present financial situation and how to stretch limited resources by preparing a balanced personal budget.

Credit Unions

These are money co-operatives run by groups of people with something in common, such as belonging to the same local organisation, church or club. They are intended to provide a way of getting credit at low cost. Members of a Credit Union save together, and the amount that they save is then available to give out as loans.

Further information about Credit Unions and how to set them up, or which ones might be in your local area, is available from:

Association of British Credit Unions Ltd
Unit 307
Westminster Business Centre
339 Kennington Lane
London SE11 5QY
Tel: 071–582 2626

National Federation of Saving and Co-operative Credit Unions
Credit Union House
102 Tong Street
Bradford
W. Yorks BD4 6HD
Tel: 0274 687692

Charities

There are a number of other organisations which may also be available to help anyone who is in severe financial difficulty. Most will expect that anyone approaching them has already tried the normal statutory sources and family connections.

There are many charities. It is necessary to identify the ones most relevant to you or your parent by way of background or individual needs. For instance, if your parent is disabled it will be better to identify a charity that is associated with that particular disability or with the disease that causes the disability.

There are a large number of charities that are set up to look after members of a particular group and their families. These include trade and professional organisations, welfare societies tied up to a particular religion such as Jewish Care (see below) or those for people with a professional or similar background such as the Distressed Gentlefolks Aid Association (see below). Finally there are national charities whose objectives are specifically identified with the needs of the elderly or disabled, such as Counsel and Care for the Elderly (see below).

Some of these organisations provide continuing support for an individual while others will only provide a one-off grant. However, once a decision is made to approach them, it is advisable to see if a doctor or local social worker can support the application.

Charitable and other organisations that might assist you include:

Charity Search
25 Portview Road
Avonmouth
Bristol BS11 9LD
Tel: 0272 824060

Charity Search is a free advisory service for elderly people in genuine financial difficulties that introduces them to charities that might help them.

The Association of Charity Officers
c/o RICS Benevolent Fund Limited
First Floor
Tavistock House North
Tavistock Square
London WC1H 9RJ
Tel: 071–383 5557
The Association keeps a directory of about 250 member charities, many of whom are professional and trade benevolent funds. They will try and assist enquirers locate sources of help.

Counsel and Care for the Elderly
Lower Ground Floor
Twyman House
16 Bonny Street
London NW1 9PG
Tel: 071–485 1566
Counsel and Care is a national service for elderly people. It provides information and advice to older persons and those concerned with their care and welfare on nearly any relevant matter. It also provides, if possible, lump sum grants to improve the quality of life of older people.

Distressed Gentlefolks Aid Association
Vicarage Gate
London W8 4AQ
Tel: 071–229 9341
This charity assists people of a professional or similar background in one of two ways. It helps them to stay at home or in a private home when they do not have the means to do so under their own resources. It also runs a number of homes offering both residential and full nursing facilities.

Jewish Care
221 Golders Green Road
London NW11 9DW
Tel: 081–458 3282
Jewish Care offers many assistance programmes including residential and nursing homes and sheltered housing schemes for Jewish people.

Society for the Assistance of Ladies in Reduced Circumstances
Lancaster House
25 Hornyold Road
Malvern
Worcs WR14 1QQ

National Benevolent Institution
61 Bayswater Road
London W2 3PG
Tel: 071–723 0021

Independent Living 1993 Fund
PO Box 183
Nottingham NG8 3RD
Tel: 0602 290423
The Fund is designed to help people who are very severely disabled to stay at home. Anyone under 65 who receives at least £200 per week from the Social Services is eligible to apply.

The Charities Aid Foundation
48 Pembury Road
Tonbridge
Kent TN9 2JD
Tel: 0732 771333

INVESTMENTS AND OTHER FINANCIAL MATTERS

Generally the desire to receive a regular income is the most important consideration for anyone who has retired or is about to retire. Most people will have contributed a sufficient amount during their working lives to receive some form of pension, and many will have accumulated some capital by the time that they retire. In the previous sections I considered the help and benefits that are available for people in need. Now I will look at some of the options for those who are better off.

Although many of the statements and facts are directly relevant to the individuals themselves who have retired or are elderly, I feel it is as important for their children or relatives to be aware of the available alternatives, in order to be able to discuss them or give advice.

I will examine the problems that face people in deciding how to invest and how to cater for their current and future needs. I will also look in general at certain types of investment and at different types of plans and schemes to provide flexibility and maintain security in old age. I will consider how investors should seek out the right advisers and what protection and compensation schemes are available to them.

None of the companies or types of investment mentioned in this book should be considered to be recommended as to its suitability. The inclusion of a name or a product of any company in this book is not an endorsement by myself of that company or product. Each individual wishing to invest or make a decision on savings must take the necessary due care, advice and diligence before proceeding with an investment. Although I can advise on what precautionary steps to take before making a decision, it must be remembered that a type of investment or saving plan suitable for one person may be totally inappropriate for another. Once the assistance of an authorised adviser has been sought, and he or she has been provided with all of the relevant information about you or your parent's affairs, he or she will supply advice. The final decision on the type of savings plan or investment then lies with the person whose money is being invested. If anyone is ever in doubt, seek another adviser.

The Choice Facing Investors

Most retired people are mainly interested in generating income and at least maintaining their capital base. But before deciding what type of investment is most likely to meet the requirements, an investor must consider four fundamental points:
1. taxation
2. risk
3. inflation
4. returns

Taxation
A saver or investor must chose a scheme of investment or saving that is appropriate to his or her tax position.

Risk
No investor should accept a higher level of risk than he or she can comfortably cope with and afford. For instance, although the stock market, which provides a higher risk than a bank deposit, may produce good returns over a long period of time, it does fluctuate and if money is needed in a hurry, the investor might have to sell when the market is at a low level.

Inflation
An investor who is concerned about the risk to his or her capital, and at the same time requires income, might wish to invest all capital into a Building Society or National Savings account. Although both the investor's criteria are met by this action, if inflation continues there is no growth allowed for in the capital to combat its effects. Even with inflation at a 25-year low, an annual income that is sufficient in 1994 will not necessarily suffice in 2004.

Returns
An investor who forgoes risk will generally expect a lower return than one who accepts an element of risk. However, in the last three years building societies have cut the rate on their monthly income accounts (still the most popular home for older people's savings) by nearly two thirds. Although the net return may still be higher than the rate of inflation, monthly income from these accounts has fallen dramatically. This has meant that many people who rely on their income from this type of saving are suffering additional hardship.

The information contained below is a summary of some of the options available. It is not intended to and should not take the place of considered professional advice that takes into account the actual requirements and the current financial situation of the investor.

Investment in Shares (directly or by other means)

Shares in Companies
Shares are issued by companies to allow that company to finance expenditure. By owning a share, an investor is entitled to participate in the performance of the business. Although the owner or shareholder will participate in profits by receiving dividends (a sharing of a portion of the company's current profits, paid at the discretion of the directors), there is no guarantee of how the company will perform or that dividends will be paid. The investor will buy the shares through a stockbroker at a given price, quoted for that day.

The share price might rise (principally if the company performs well) or it might fall. Although investors can never lose more than they invest (assuming they avoid the very high risk areas of option and futures trading) it is possible to lose the whole value of the investment if, for example, the company is put into liquidation.

The value of shares fluctuates, sometimes wildly. One of the primary principles to be followed by investors when making any form of investment is the need to spread the risk. If investors put all of their money into only one or two shares (a course of action that is strictly *not* recommended), the overall performance of their portfolio is purely tied to those shares; even though the overall market is increasing strongly, their shares might be falling in value.

Those with large amounts of money to invest are able to spread the risk by investing in a wide range of shares.

For the smaller investor there are more suitable means of investing in the performance of companies. Investment trusts and unit trusts, explained below, provide vehicles by which investors can participate in the stock market without being exposed to the type of risk that is involved in investing directly into shares. The reason for this is that, indirectly, the investor has a wide spread of investment. However, neither type of trust is without risk, and some more specialist trusts carry a higher degree of risk than others. Investment in this manner is more suited to the long term.

Investment Trusts
Investment Trusts are companies formed purely to deal in other companies' shares. They issue shares themselves, which may be bought and sold easily through stockbrokers. An investment in one of these Trusts represents an indirect investment in the wide range of businesses that they have invested in. However, investment trusts are allowed to borrow money and to use it to invest in other concerns. This 'gearing' tends to enhance the value of the shares in a rising market and depress the value in a falling market. Therefore, the share price of investment trusts can be very volatile.

Unit Trusts
Unit Trusts also invest in shares in the same way as investment trusts. However, rather than buying shares in a company traded on the Stock Exchange, the investor purchases units in a group of investments that are actively managed by a fund manager. Usually twice a year the unit holder will be allocated a dividend, called a 'distribution', based on the units held. Either a cheque will be paid or the managers will buy more units for the holder, depending upon whether he or she holds 'Income' or 'Accumulation' units.

Unit trust prices are quoted in the newspapers and do not have to be bought through the Stock Exchange; you may simply contact the managers direct. The names, addresses and telephone numbers of the managers are always quoted above the prices in the newspapers.

Personal Equity Plans—PEPs
PEPs allow individuals to invest up to £6,000 every financial year into Equities, Unit Trusts or Investment Trusts provided certain conditions are adhered to. In

addition to this general PEP, it is also possible to invest £3,000 into a 'single company' PEP. Further information about PEPs can be obtained from specialist PEP managers; most of the banks and large financial institutions offer a PEP service. These are well advertised, particularly towards the end of the tax year.

All income from dividends and interest earned within the PEP is tax-free, and the proceeds are free of Capital Gains.

Fixed Income Investments
The safest schemes for savings and investment come from the Banks, Building Societies and National Savings.

Banks and Building Societies
Both banks and building societies have a wide range of savings schemes. Regular interest is paid on capital, but there is no chance of making a capital gain.

Interest is normally credited to an account after deduction of tax. It is possible, and advisable, for a non-taxpayer to request that the interest is credited gross. To do this it is necessary to complete Inland Revenue Form R85 (available from all banks, building societies and tax offices).

The rates and terms of deposits vary widely. The larger the sum invested and the longer the period this sum is committed for, the greater may be the rate of interest. However, all investors should consider with what regularity the interest will be paid and also for how long they are willing to lock their money into an account. Although money can always be withdrawn from a long-term savings account, there is normally a financial penalty for doing so.

National Savings
All National Savings schemes, including even Premium Bonds, offer total security for the capital invested. There are many types of product available and the full range is detailed in the National Savings product leaflet available at most post offices. Income Bonds are more suitable for investors who pay no tax, whereas National Savings Certificates and Index-linked Certificates are more suitable for higher rate taxpayers.

Tax Exempt Special Savings Accounts—TESSA
Recently introduced by the Government, TESSAs enable people to place up to £9,000 over five years (£3,000 in the first year, £1,800 in the subsequent four years) into a deposit account where, after the five-year qualifying period, the gross interest may be paid free of tax. Net interest may be withdrawn during the five-year period, but withdrawal of capital will disqualify the TESSA.

Government Stock (Gilts)
Gilts are issued by the Government to finance expenditure. They are a mixture of National Savings schemes and shares in companies; like National Savings they are backed by the Government, but like shares their value can rise and fall.

Gilts are fixed-term stock with a guaranteed fixed interest rate. As interest rates increase and decrease the capital value of the Gilt also fluctuates because the fixed interest rate is always based on the nominal value of the Gilt. Therefore, a Gilt issued for maturity in 1998 with an interest rate of 12 per cent might be quoted at £118, as opposed to its nominal value of £100. This indicates that interest rates are currently lower than 12 per cent (as the capital value of the Gilt is higher than £100). If the Gilt was bought at £118, the gross yield would approximate 10 per cent.

Gilts can be bought through a stockbroker or through the Post Office. The Post Office will not give advice as to which Gilts to buy, but the National Savings leaflet, *Government Stock* gives general information on Gilts.

Insurance Scheme Investments

Income and Growth Bonds
Income and growth bonds consist of portfolios of Investment Bonds held in a range of Equity, Fixed Interest and Cash Funds managed by leading investment institutions. In many respects they are similar to unit trusts, although care should be taken when investing in them because no basic rate tax is reclaimable on the dividends paid (despite the fact that they are paid 'net') and liquidation of the bonds may lead to a tax liability at one of the higher rates of tax.

Guaranteed Equity Funds—GEFs
GEFs allow individuals, who consider the inherent risk in investing in shares or unit and investment trusts to be too great, to invest into equities.

In return for accepting a guarantee that the price of the original investment will not fall below a certain level and that the price of the fund will move in line with a pre-selected Index (such as the FT-SE 100 Index), the investor forgoes most of the dividend income from the underlying investments and also the potential to perform better than the market.

However, each GEF should be looked at carefully: some are better if markets rise in a straight line but lose out if the market has begun to fall when they are to be sold. Other GEFs guard against this by averaging out returns in a predetermined period before they mature.

Guaranteed Income Bonds—GIBs
GIBs provide a fixed, guaranteed income over a period with a guaranteed return of capital. Although the rate will usually be a little lower than long-term deposits in a Building Society, the overall yield will remain constant. GIBs provide no hedge against inflation.

Guaranteed Acceptance Policies
Some companies are now selling 'guaranteed acceptance' policies, which are aimed at pensioners and people over 50. These policies, which are generally non-profit whole-life plans, offer a fixed amount of lifetime insurance cover without the insured needing to undergo any form of medical examination or answer any medical questions.

They are protection plans rather than savings plans, and are aimed at people who believe that they are either too old for a normal policy or that medicals will be too detailed and onerous for them. They have been very popular in recent years. However, if a person is in reasonable health, he or she should have no problem taking out an ordinary non-profit whole-life policy, which would give much better value for money.

Annuities

To buy an annuity one pays an insurance company a lump sum, in return for which the insurance company pays a guaranteed income for life or for a specified period. Therefore, annuities are suitable for people at or near retirement age, because the younger you are when you buy an annuity, the longer your life expectancy will be and, consequently, the lower will be the annual income paid.

It is possible to buy escalation annuities which increase by a fixed per cent per annum, or inflation-linked annuities. The purpose of these is that the buying power of the income paid is not constantly diminished with time and inflation. These types of annuity are more expensive and pay less income per pound of annuity purchased in the early years.

'With Profit' Endowment Policies

The maximum age for endowment policies is 65, so they are more suited to those about to retire and in good health who wish to save for a capital sum which will be received tax-free after 10 years. These policies are generally low risk, except anyone wanting to sell or surrender the policy before maturity will lose a substantial portion of the terminal value of the policy.

If it is necessary to dispose of them early, it is best to try and sell them through a recognised broker rather than surrender them. Your financial adviser will put you in touch with one of these brokers. Any policies encashed within the first four years of their existence will almost certainly not even recoup the value of the money invested.

Further Reading

Investing for Beginners, Daniel O'Shea (Financial Times Business Information), £11.50

Managing a Lump Sum—a free booklet from Help the Aged (address page 49) which explains in simple language the different types of investments available, translates some investment jargon and describes the choices open to anyone wishing to invest or save.

Thinking about Money—a free booklet from Help the Aged which explains how to assess the current situation and prepare a personal balanced budget.

Your Taxes and Savings 1993–94, Jennie Hawthorne and Sally West (Age Concern), £4.50

This book provides information about the wide range of investment opportunities available. The section on tax explains how the tax system affects people over retirement age, including how to avoid paying more than necessary. (See also Chapter 7 of this book.)

Which? Way to Save and Invest (Consumers Association), £10.95

Approaching Retirement (Consumers Association), £6.95

Consumers Association
2 Marylebone Road
London NW1 4DF
Tel: 071–486 5544

The following organisations also produce free publications on their respective types of savings and investments:

Banking Information Service
10 Lombard Street
London EC3V 9AT
Tel: 071–626 8486

Building Societies Association
3 Savile Row
London W1X 1AF
Tel: 071–437 0655

Association of British Insurers
51 Gresham Street
London EC2V 7HQ
Tel: 071–600 3333
For information on insurance-linked schemes.

Association of Investment Trust Companies
Sixth Floor
Park House
16 Finsbury Circus
London EC2M 7JJ
Tel: 071–588 5347

Department for National Savings
Marketing and Sales Information Dept
Charles House
375 Kensington High Street
London W14 8SD
(Also available from major post offices)

The Stock Exchange
Public Affairs Department
The London Stock Exchange
London EC2N 1HP

Unit Trust Association Information Unit
65 Kingsway
London WC2D 6TD

Money Education, operating as Money Management Council
PO Box 77
Hertford
Herts SG14 2HW
Tel: 0992 503448
Money Education is an independent impartial charity that promotes education and better understanding in personal and family finance. It does not offer individual advice but produces free leaflets, available from the above address. Send an A4-sized sae. Its factsheets include:

No 1 *You and Your Money (A General Introduction)*

No 2 *Savings and Lump Sum Investment*

Where Can You Find Financial Advice?

It is important to ensure that anyone seeking financial advice will receive the very best professional advice. However, it is hard to know where to find a reliable adviser who will give investment advice that is entirely suitable for your needs, or those of your parent or relative.

As a simple rule of thumb, potential investors must consider that the more they are prepared to take a risk with their investment, the more important it is to seek professional financial advice. For instance, if one is placing money on deposit in a bank, it is sufficient to identify the best rate of interest for the amount being deposited. However, if one wishes to invest in the stock market or to buy an annuity, one needs to have advice on all of the different options and types of investment that are available.

There are many sources for professional financial advice. Since the Financial Services Act 1986 the markets have become more regulated, and anyone providing advice on financial matters has to be authorised by one of a number of bodies. The authorisation procedure is intended to identify individuals and organisations which are not fit and proper to act in a professional capacity within the financial markets that are controlled or monitored by those bodies.

The relevant organisations are listed below. Further details of the protection that is offered to investors is provided in the section on 'General Investor Protection' (page 129). Each of these organisations will provide anyone free of charge with a list of members within his or her particular area of the UK.

Securities and Investments Board
Gavrelle House
2–14 Bunhill Row
London EC1Y 8RA
Tel: 071–638 1240

The SIB, which is responsible for controlling the four Self Regulatory Organisations (SROs) listed below, has a comprehensive list of all authorised firms and individual advisers.

It also produces a number of free booklets:
The Background to Investor Protection
Investment Businesses: What to Do If You Need to Complain
The Central Register
Compensation for Investors
How to Spot the Investment Cowboys

Self Regulatory Organisations (SROs)

FIMBRA (Financial Intermediaries, Managers and Brokers Regulatory Association)
Hertsmere House
Hertsmere Road
London E14 4AB
Tel: 071–538 8860

FIMBRA regulates the *independent* intermediaries advising on life assurance, pensions, unit trusts, stocks and shares and financial management. This is the most important organisation for the majority of individual investors.

IMRO (the Investment Management Regulatory Organisation)
Broadwalk House
Appold Street
London EC2A 2LL
Tel: 071–628 6022
IMRO regulates investment managers, including unit trust managers and trustees.

LAUTRO (the Life Assurance and Unit Trust Regulatory Organisation)
Centre Point
103 New Oxford Street
London WC1 1QH
Tel: 071–538 8860
LAUTRO regulates the marketing of life assurance, pensions and unit trust products.

SFA (the Securities and Futures Authority Ltd)
The Stock Exchange Building
Old Broad Street
London EC2A 2LL
Tel: 071–256 9000
SFA is responsible for the regulation of those who advise on and deal in shares dealt on the Stock Exchange as well as trading in futures and options. It also covers advisers whose secondary activities are advising on and dealing in unit trusts, futures, investment management and similar investments.

Recognised Professional Bodies
In addition to the SROs, there are a number of other organisations called Recognised Professional Bodies (RPBs). These regulate, for example, insurance brokers, solicitors and accountants who have obtained authorisation to give advice on investments through their professional body.

Here are the names, addresses and telephone numbers of the five main RPBs:

ACCA (Chartered Association of Certified Accountants)
29 Lincoln's Inn Fields
London WC2A 3EE
Tel: 071–242 6855

IBRC (Insurance Brokers' Registration Council)
15 St Helen's Place
London EC3A 6DS
Tel: 071–588 4387

ICAEW (Institute of Chartered Accountants in England and Wales)
PO Box 433
Chartered Accountants Hall
Moorgate Place
London EC2P 2BJ
Tel: 071–628 7060

Law Societies

Law Society of England and Wales
113 Chancery Lane
London WC1 1PL
Tel: 071–242 1222

Law Society of Scotland
The Law Society's Hall
26 Drumsheugh Gardens
Edinburgh EH3 7YR
Tel: 031–226 7411

Other Organisations

IFAP (IFA Promotion Ltd)
Fourth Floor
28 Greville Street
London EC1N 8SU
Tel: 071–831 4027
IFAP is a commercial company which promotes Independent Financial Advisers (IFAs). Over 4,000 firms around the country are registered with IFAP. Telephone 0483 461461 for a free list of independent financial advisers near your home or work area. IFAP will also send out a booklet called *Your Guide to Independent Financial Advice* which details, among other things, the type of questions that should be asked by anyone seeking advice from an IFA.

Association of British Insurers
51 Gresham Street
London EC2V 7HO
Tel: 071–600 3333
The Association mainly deals with property and contents type of insurance as opposed to life assurance. It produces a range of leaflets on many general aspects of insurance (send sae please), in particular to help people consider the adequacy of their cover. It also gives helpful advice on how to calculate the amount of cover that should be taken for a property, depending upon its size and location.

BIIBA (British Insurance and Investment Brokers' Association)
BIIBA House
14 Bevis Marks
London EC3A 7NT
Provides a list of brokers and consultants

The Money Management Council (address page 124) also provides two relevant factsheets free of charge (if by post please send an A4-sized sae): *Where Can I Get Financial Advice?* and *Watch Out for Fraud.*

Types of Adviser and Advice

In the past few years, as financial markets have become more complex and individuals have tended to become wealthier with more substantial net assets, more people have sought, or have tried to seek, impartial and expert advice. With the

127

distinctions made after the Financial Services Act 1986 it has become easier to identify the type of advice that one is seeking.

There are now two types of financial adviser:

1. The 'tied' agent, who is linked to a particular company or group of companies which sell financial products. He or she acts on behalf of the sellers of the product and will offer advice based on their product range; he or she need not compare the quality of the product with others in the marketplace.
2. The Independent Financial Adviser (IFA), who is totally independent and therefore by definition should also be impartial. He or she acts on behalf of the buyer of the product (the investor) and should be in a position to offer the best advice from the whole marketplace; when advising he or she should compare the products of a number of companies before identifying the best product for the client. IFAs are legally bound to obtain specific information about their clients' financial and general circumstances; therefore the more information they have, the better can be the quality of the advice.

All Independent Financial Advisers (IFAs) must be authorised by an approved body, such as FIMBRA. Many insurance brokers, accountants and solicitors will have obtained authorisation through their own professional organisations, called Recognised Professional Bodies (RPBs, see above).

If an adviser indicates that he or she is a member of LAUTRO, that adviser will certainly be a tied agent.

There is no right answer to the question of whether to consult a 'tied' or 'independent' adviser; either may give entirely suitable advice. However, investors should always be clear about which they are dealing with, and accept that if the adviser is 'tied' he or she will be investing money only in the company to which he or she is tied.

Having decided which they prefer, investors should ensure that their adviser is registered with FIMBRA or any other relevant organisation. Investors should meet their broker face to face; it is easier to understand something explained in a meeting than over a telephone where examples cannot be shown.

After the meeting, a written summary of what is being offered should always be requested. If there is anything that remains unclear, answers should be obtained in writing. The broker must be fully briefed on all of the investor's circumstances; the broker has, by law, to give advice suitable only to the circumstances of the investor.

The advice received by an investor will not come free; both types of adviser are likely to be paid a commission on the sale of the investment products. Some may charge investors a fee, a proportion of which they may get back if the adviser then receives a commission from an insurance firm. It is always worth remembering that some forms of investment and types of company pay more of a commission than others.

Investors may want to check with their adviser that the advice being given is the most suitable for them and not just generating the highest commission for the adviser. It is therefore quite reasonable to ask an adviser what commission he or she will be receiving on each type of investment; the adviser is also bound by law to provide the information asked for.

Before deciding whether an adviser is suitable, the following questions at least should have been asked and satisfactorily answered:

ASK THE ADVISER
1. Are you independent or tied?
2. By which body are you authorised?
3. How long have you been in the business of providing financial advice, and in what areas do you specialise?
4. What commission will you receive on the products that you are offering?
5. How are my interests best protected?

ASK YOURSELF/YOUR PARENT
1. Does the adviser appear to know what he or she is doing, and does he or she show sufficient specialised knowledge about the investments being recommended?
2. Does the adviser show an interest in my business and would my interests come before his or her own?
3. Do I feel comfortable with the adviser, do I understand the fees and charges and will he or she provide continuity of service?
4. Is the adviser legitimately carrying on business?

General Investor Protection

The Financial Services Act 1986 has ushered in a formidable body of legislation that is designed, among other things, to protect the interests of private investors and ensure that they receive impartial professional advice. This has been done by enforcing stringent controls over companies operating within the financial services industry.

Enforcement of the regulations is controlled by the Securities and Investment Board. This organisation delegates authority to various bodies called Self Regulatory Organisations (SROs). A list of these, with telephone numbers and addresses, was given on pages 125–126.

It is the SROs' responsibility to ensure that all their members comply with the complex conduct of Business Rules. Under certain circumstances compensation is provided to private investors in the case of failure of member firms, and also of the investors. The SROs have recourse to the appropriate body in case of complaint.

Current legislation restricts the type of business that companies can carry on, and ensures that they are qualified to carry on professionally the businesses for which they do receive authorisation. There are four main areas of investment specialisation which can be authorised:
1. Advising on investments
2. Arranging and transacting Life, Pension and Unit Trust contracts
3. Arranging and transacting other types of investment
4. Managing investments

The four main SROs, again, are:
- Financial Intermediaries, Managers and Brokers Regulatory Association—(FIMBRA)
- the Investment Management Regulatory Organisation—(IMRO)
- the Life Assurance and Unit Trust Regulatory Organisation—(LAUTRO)
- the Securities and Futures Authority Ltd—(SFA).

For investors to be sure that their investment adviser is registered, they can contact the SIB and check its Central Register, which contains a computerised database of 40,000 investment firms. The Register contains details of the firm's authorised status, by whom the firm is regulated, whether it is authorised to handle clients' money or merely to give advice, and in what types of investment business it is permitted to engage. The public can gain access to the Register by writing to, visiting or telephoning the SIB.

Securities and Investments Board
Gavrelle House
2–14 Bunhill Row
London EC1Y 8RA
Tel: 071–929 3652

It is also possible to access the Register through the Telecom Gold or Prestel on-line public networks, which are also available in a number of libraries and Citizens Advice Bureaux. The Register is accessed through the Prestel service by keying in *SIB# or *301#. Apart from the charges made by the provider of a publicly available on-line system, the on-line access to the Register costs 44p per minute plus 75p per name checked (and is subject to change).

Compensation
The act of investing nearly always means that one has to let someone else handle one's money. This means that financial advice businesses give advice, may receive cheques from investors for the investment and also may receive the proceeds of the sale of the investment. There are rules in place to ensure that investors' money is duly segregated from the business' own funds but, even if reasonable precautions are taken, there is always a very remote chance that something may go wrong: the money might be lost as a result of fraud or owing to the company going bankrupt without having protected its clients' money properly.

When this happens, there are compensation schemes in place for people who have lost their money as a result of an investment company undertaking their business improperly. However, for these schemes to be operative it is essential that the investment company is either recognised by the Securities and Investment Board (SIB) or is a bank, building society or life insurance company (which have their own compensation schemes, governed by the Deposit Protection Board and the Policy Holders Protection Scheme respectively).

Further information can be obtained from the SIB and its Self Regulatory Organisations about the scope of compensation available if one of their members goes bankrupt. *Remember: Investment can be a risky business; no one will pay investors compensation if their investment falls in value or inflation erodes the real value of the return.*

The Investors Compensation Fund

This Fund is carried out by a company separate from the SIB. It may be able to help investors if all of the following apply to their position:

- the investors are private investors
- the investment firm is fully authorised
- the firm is unable to pay out investors' claims
- the firm owes the investors money, or is holding shares or other investments on their behalf
- the investors' claims arise out of business regulated by the Financial Services Act.

If you are uncertain about the definitions used, the SIB will be able to assist if you write to them or telephone on 071–929 3652.

In addition, they produce an explanatory booklet, *Compensation for Investors*, which they will send to you free of charge (address page 130).

A claimant receives the first £30,000 of a claim in full, along with 90 per cent of the next £20,000. Therefore anyone claiming £50,000 would receive a maximum amount of £48,000.

Banks and Building Societies

In the event of a bank or building society failing, there are compensation schemes which protect 75 per cent of the money lodged in a bank up to £20,000 (£15,000 in total per bank) or 90 per cent of the money lodged in a building society up to £20,000 (£18,000 in total per building society).

Financial Planning to Pay for a Nursing Home

At some stage older parents or relatives might have to go and live in a residential or nursing home. This can produce one of the largest expenses of their lives, and can create genuine financial problems. Whereas savings are made for retirement, for most people these are insufficient to cover such large expenditures as nursing home fees.

For those who are less well off, the new Community Care arrangements that came into force in April 1993 stipulate that a person who may need help should first contact the local authority's Social Services Department (see Chapter 4, page 65). Each local authority sets a standard charge, being the amount it is prepared to pay for accommodation in the homes within its area. The local authority will assess the resident's ability to pay for the home by using the regulations of The National Assistance (Assessment of Resources) Regulation 1992.

This means-test is similar to that used by the Government to assess eligibility for Income Support. Depending upon a person's circumstances, he or she may be offered a placement by the local authority in a home where that authority has a contract. If that is the case, the amount payable for the home will not be more than the standard charge set by the local authority. However, the individual will have to contribute an amount that the local authority deem he or she is able to pay; the local authority will pay the difference.

Residents are entitled to Income Support at the basic rate, as well as a residential allowance, but only if their capital is less than £8,000. They will not be entitled to any more benefits. More information is available earlier in this chapter and in DSS leaflet IS50, *Help If You Live in a Residential Care Home or Nursing Home*.

It is possible for an individual to enter a private home without recourse to the local authority. If this is the case it may be possible to claim allowances such as Attendance Allowance. For further details see page 105 of this chapter. However, if an individual's savings are limited, it is always sensible to approach the local authority first.

If assistance is not available from the local authority, or if an individual wishes to live in more expensive accommodation, consideration must be given to using other resources. Below I list several organisations that may be able to help and give advice, and consider some ways of providing funding for private homes.

Specialist Organisations

Asset Financial Planning
Freepost (BS2614)
PO Box 106
37 Broad Street
Bristol BS99 7YJ
Tel: 0272 263822
Asset, part of National Westminster Insurance Services, has a financial planning service that was devised in conjunction with Age Concern. Asset is able to advise on a range of topics concerning the elderly, in addition to the healthcare plans.

Eagle Star Life Assurance Company Ltd
Eagle Star House
Bath Road
Cheltenham
Glos GL53 7LQ
Tel: 0242 221311
Eagle Star has a specialist Care Fees Payment Plan, which is designed to meet many of the worries that are associated with paying for long-term care. In return for a lump sum payment, usually funded from savings or the sale of a property, it guarantees a series of payments designed to meet care fees as they become due.

Nursing Home Fees Agency
Old Bank House
95 London Road
Headington
Oxford OX3 9AE
Tel: 0865 750665
The NHFA advises potential residents of care homes and their relatives on how best to provide for long-term care fees from resources available, with an aim to protect capital and preserve the ability to pay fees. They will also advise on a care home resident's entitlement and claims for DSS and local authority entitlements.

Raising Capital from One's Home

For many people, their principal asset is their home. This has probably been acquired throughout their years of working when they had a reasonable disposable income. After retirement, this income is likely to drop considerably, especially in later years, unless there is an element of inflation-linking in their pension rights.

Many elderly homeowners find themselves in the unenviable position of having insufficient income on which to live while the principal value of what they own is locked up in their house. The only apparent option to many would be to sell their home to raise 'income producing' capital.

However, over 20 years ago a scheme was devised which allowed homeowners to release regular income from the capital tied up in their home while remaining *in situ*. These plans are called Home Income Plans. They are made up from several alternative types of scheme, all of which purport to achieve the same objective. Recent experience has shown that some types of plan are less safe and secure than others. As a result of this, a group of the main specialist providers of Home Income Plans throughout the UK have collectively launched a Code of Practice called *SHIP*—Safe Home Income Plans.

The Code requires companies to provide a fair, simple and complete presentation of their plans and, as a further safeguard, stipulates that the solicitors of a person entering a plan must sign a certificate before proceeding with the plan, to acknowledge that the essential features and implications of the chosen SHIP Plan have been brought to their attention. All companies that are bound by the SHIP Code will carry a SHIP logo. Further details of the Code are available from:

SHIP Campaign
Hinton & Wild (Home Plans) Ltd
374 Ewell Road, Surbiton
Surrey KT6 7BB
Tel: 081–390 8166

Most plans involve either raising a loan against the value of the home, or selling all or part of the property. From the proceeds of the money raised an annuity is bought which can provide guaranteed income for life. Both types of plan are acceptable; which one is most suitable depends upon the circumstances of each individual. All those considering a plan must consider whether they will retain security of tenure in their home for the reminder of their life, whether they will have the freedom to move house if they wish and whether they will receive a cash sum or an assured regular income.

There is generally a minimum age for people to be able to participate in the plans. This varies from plan to plan and may depend upon whether an individual is single or married; it is generally between 63 and 70.

Some of the types of plan available are:
• home reversion schemes
• investment bond income schemes
• roll up loans.

Home Reversion Schemes

Under this your parents' home is sold to the 'reversion' company, but they (or either surviving partner) retain the legal right to live as tenants for life. They receive a percentage of the value of the home outright; it is not a loan. Typically the amount received is less than 50 per cent of the value of the property. It is not necessary to sell title to all of the home. From these schemes it is possible to link the income generated from the capital raised to the value of the property in future years.

Investment Bond Income Schemes

With an investment bond income scheme, money is advanced by a building society, with the home as security. The loan raised is invested in an investment bond, with the expectation that its appreciation will be sufficient to repay the loan and provide extra income. These types of schemes were marketed very aggressively in the late 1980s, but stock market performance in recent years has failed to meet expectations and, combined with the fall in property values, has resulted in many homes being placed in jeopardy. These schemes are generally unsuitable for older homeowners, and many of them have been banned by FIMBRA and LAUTRO.

Roll Up Loans

This plan entails a loan being taken out against the security of the home; capital and income repayments may be deferred and the interest is added to the loan month by month. When interest rates are high (at about 15 per cent), the accumulation of interest will mean that the loan will double about every five years. If house prices are also falling, there is a danger that the home will provide insufficient security for the loan.

Useful Contacts

Age Alliance
6 Allerton Hill
Leeds LS7 3QB
Tel: 0532 370666
Age Alliance assists retired homeowners to raise a tax-free lump sum *without risk* by selling part or all of their property equity. They continue to live in their home and receive guaranteed lifetime occupancy arranged through their own solicitor. There are no repayments or interest. The money can be spent or invested in any way.

Home and Capital Trust Limited
31 Goldington Road
Bedford MK 40 3LH
Tel: 0234 340511
Home and Capital Trust, a member of SHIP, specialises in providing a cash lump sum through the sale of all or part of a property, while retaining for the owner a lifetime rent-free occupancy.

Allchurches Life Assurance Ltd
Beaufort House
Brunswick Road
Gloucester GL1 1JZ
Tel: 0452 503456
A member of SHIP

Carlyle Life Assurance Company Ltd
21 Windsor Place
Cardiff CF1 3BY
Tel: 0222 371726
A member of SHIP

Investment Property Reversions Ltd
34 Hill Crest Road
Purley
Surrey CR8 2JE
Tel: 081–645 9444

Home for Life (Properties) Limited
10–12 Spencer Road
West Green
Crawley
Sussex RH11 7DA
Tel: 081–343 9666

Further Reading
Using Your Home As Capital, Cecil Hinton (Age Concern, 1993), £4.50 including p&p.

Updated every year, this explains the different types of Home Income Plan available as well as their advantages and disadvantages. It also provides a check-list of matters everyone should consider before taking up a plan. (See page 48 for Age Concern details.)

Age Concern also produce a factsheet (No 24) called *Housing Schemes for Older People Where a Capital Sum is Required*. This provides information for many of the older people who want to move home, own their own property or have other assets such as savings, but often do not have enough to buy outright and cannot find suitable rented accommodation.

Your Money in Retirement, Paul Lewis (The Homeowners Friendly Society), £2.99.
An easy-to-understand guide providing advice in pre-retirement planning, pensions and safe ways to take money from one's home. Available from:

The Homeowners Friendly Society
Freepost 2153
Shadwell Lane
Leeds LS17 7YY

Insurance as Part of an Overall Financial Plan

Throughout our lives we tend to take out insurance, whether it is because we are compelled to, such as for a car, or to obtain peace of mind in case of disaster or loss. Everyone must balance up the cost of insurance against the impact of not being insured in the event of a disaster.

For instance, long-term care insurance should be considered: if you or your parent had to have full-time care because of an unexpected illness or disability the cost could be substantial and easily outweigh the price of paying regular annual premiums. Therefore I believe that consideration should be given to all aspects of insurance available to the older person, as a integral part of his or her financial planning.

Older people have, in recent years, been specifically targeted for certain types of insurance. Companies specialise in insurance for those aged 50 and over for a wide range of cover, which includes health, travel, car and household insurance. Often the rates available from these specialist companies are much more competitive than from standard sources (see also 'Travel Insurance' in Chapter 5, page 91).

Insurance brings the knowledge that, should a crisis occur, you would be able to fall back on the insurance company for assistance. As people insure against death, terminal illness or dread disease to ensure that their dependants will not suffer undue financial burden upon their death or inability to work, so it is now possible to insure against the need for long-term care. During the early 1990s a new type of policy, called long-term Care Insurance, was introduced into the UK by several companies. This insurance pays out in the event of long-term disability or illness and helps provide protection for savings and assets which might otherwise be used up to pay for care.

It is advisable to consider all of the different types of insurance available, and to review policies each year to ensure that they are either adequate or not vastly in excess of requirements. The names of some specialist companies are provided below.

Special Insurance Cover for Older People

WPA (Western Provident Association)
Rivergate House
Blackbrook Park
Taunton
Somerset TA1 2PE
Tel: 0823 623330
WPA, a not-for-profit organisation, offers a range of health insurance schemes for the over-60s. These schemes qualify for tax relief. They are Beech, Senior Maple, Walnut and Senior Elect. In addition a 'Home Independence' policy is available which provides cover for nursing and care services at home following a stay in hospital.

Age Concern Insurance Services
Garrod House
Chaldon Road
Caterham
Surrey CR3 5YZ
Tel: 0883 346964
Provide a range of general insurance for the older person.

CGA Direct
Freepost
Horsham
W. Sussex RH12 1ZA
Tel: 0800 525200
Specialist insurance for the older person.

Exeter Friendly Society (formerly Exeter Hospital Aid Society)
Beech Hill House
Walnut Gardens
Exeter EX4 4DG
Tel: 0392 498063
Provide over-50s medical insurance.

Commercial Union Assurance Company Ltd
Third Age Initiative
Finance House
Stokes Croft
Bristol BS1 3QY
Tel: 0800 100 155
Provide long-term care insurance and well-being insurance.

Private Patients Plan
Senior Health Plan
Freepost
PPP House
Upperton Road
Eastbourne
East Sussex BN21 1BR
Tel: 0800 335555
Low-cost medical insurance with guaranteed acceptance; no age limit and no medical check-up required.

Sun Alliance Insurance
Freepost 1967
Horsham
W. Sussex RH12 1XX
Tel: 0800 300800
Offer special insurance for the over-50s called 'Motorist 50+' and 'Home-owners 50+'.

Saga Services Ltd
Saga Group
Middelburg Square
Folkestone
Kent CT20 1AZ
Tel: 0800 414525
Provide specialist insurance for the older person, covering household, medical, nursing care, convalescent care, accident and life.

Other Helpful Organisations

Advisory & Brokerage Services Ltd
Southampton House
317 High Holborn
London WC1V 7NL
Tel: 071–405 8535

Colombus Financial Advisers Limited
10 High Street
East Grinstead
W. Sussex RH19 3AW
Tel: 0342 322333

Hargreaves Lansdown Asset Management Ltd
Embassy House
Clifton
Bristol BS8 1SB
Tel: 0272 767 767

Hill Samuel Financial Services Ltd
NLA Tower
12–16 Addiscombe Road
Croydon CR9 6BP
Tel: 071–628 8011

Holmwoods Life & Pensions Limited
Centurion House
24 Monument Street
London EC3R 8AJ
Tel: 071–816 0661

Independent Financial Partnership Ltd
Windsor Court
Clarence Drive
Harrogate HG1 2PE
Tel: 0423 523311

Investors Management Services Ltd
St James House
Wellington Road North
Stockport
Cheshire SK4 2RT

Knight Williams & Co. Ltd
161 New Bond Street
London W1Y 0LA
Tel: 071–408 1138

Towry Law Financial Planning Ltd
Freepost
Newbury
Berks RG13 1BR
Tel: 0800 521196

Whitechurch Securities Limited
Freepost
Bristol BS9 2BR
Tel: 0272 687277
Retirement income specialists.

Life Insurance for Older People

General Accident
Lifecover Plus
Freepost (LE5732)
Leicester LE4 5ZA
Tel: 0800 616155
Provides affordable life assurance for those over 50; in some cases guaranteed without medical check-ups.

The Equitable Life
Freepost
Walton Street
Aylesbury
Bucks HP21 7BR
Tel: 0296 26226

Equity & Law Life Assurance Society plc
20 Lincoln's Inn Fields
London WC2A 3ES
Tel: 071–242 6844

Friends Provident Life Office
Pixham End
Dorking
Surrey RH4 1QA

Scottish Equitable Life Assurances
28 St Andrew Square
Edinburgh EH2 1YF
Tel: 031–556 9101

Unit Trusts and Other Savings Plans

Barclays Unicorn Limited
54 Lombard Street
London EC3P 3AH
Tel: 071–376 3476

Equitable Unit Trust Managers Ltd
4 Coleman Street
London EC2R 5AP
Tel: 071–606 6611

Save & Prosper Group Ltd
Freepost
Romford RM1 1BR
Tel: 071–588 1717

**Scottish Amicable Unit Trust
Managers**
150 St Vincent Street
Glasgow G2 5NQ
Tel: 041–248 2323

LEGAL AND TAX MATTERS

Help with Understanding Powers of Attorney,
Wills, Getting Out of Debt, Taxation

THIS CHAPTER CONSIDERS the implications of various legal and taxation problems that need to be considered as both you and your parents grow older.

Many people are unaware of the legal complications that may arise after the death of someone who has failed to make a will. Indeed, problems can arise even if a will *has* been made but no consideration has been given to changes in legislation (taxation, etc.) or the existing circumstances of the person making the will.

Even less consideration is given to the implications of a sickness or accident temporarily or permanently incapacitating someone to the extent that he or she is powerless to make or carry out even normal day-to-day decisions and actions.

POWERS OF ATTORNEY

A Power of Attorney is a legal document that can be given to an older child, a partner or any third party. It provides them with the authority to manage the financial and general affairs of the donor (the person making or giving the Power) in the event of sickness or incapacity. The Power of Attorney is conferred by completing a special legal document, which is available from stationers who supply legal forms or from any solicitor. Normally the document should be completed with the help of a solicitor.

Until recently an ordinary Power of Attorney was invalidated in the event of the donor no longer having the mental capacity to manage his or her own affairs. In 1986 legislation was passed which enables an Attorney, subject to certain conditions and safeguards, to be appointed against this possibility. A special form (available from the same sources as a normal Power of Attorney) must be completed and will provide what is known as an Enduring Power of Attorney.

An Enduring Power of Attorney allows the donors, while still mentally capable of deciding for themselves, to select who should act for them in the case of loss of mental capability. Subsequent legal protection is provided to ensure that the Powers conferred are not abused by the Attorney (see below).

It is advisable for anyone wishing to provide an Enduring Power of Attorney to consult with a legal adviser before completing it. Although it is obviously sensible to give one, consideration should also be given to restricting its Powers. The donor should realise that if the Powers are not limited, the Attorney is able to use the Power of Attorney for any purpose without restriction, including making gifts to him- or herself and his or her family.

It is possible to give specific Powers that are restricted or conditional (e.g. the house may not be sold, or it may only be sold under certain specified circumstances). It is also possible to appoint a number of Attorneys under different Powers to carry out specific duties or actions on behalf of the donor.

Once the Attorney, who is appointed under an Enduring Power of Attorney, believes that the donor is becoming confused or incapable, he or she must notify the donor and certain near relatives of the donor and then should apply to register the Enduring Power of Attorney with the Court of Protection.

The Court of Protection
Stewart House
24 Kingsway
London WC2B 6JX
Tel: 071–269 7000

The Court of Protection is an office of the Supreme Court. Its function is to protect and manage the financial affairs and property of people who, because of mental disorder, are unable to manage for themselves.

If there are any objections to the registration, the Court will arbitrate. The Court's control is regulated by the Mental Health Act 1983 and the Court of Protection Rules Act 1984.

The Protection Division of the Public Trust Office, on behalf of the Court, deals with the management of the affairs of the person under protection in conjunction with a Receiver appointed by the Court. Generally, in the case of an Enduring Power of Attorney, the receiver will automatically be the Attorney selected by the donor.

Considering how many people over the age of 65 suffer from senile dementia, the Act with its in-built safeguards offers a very helpful way of administering the affairs of elderly people who are unable to do so themselves.

The Public Trust Office has an excellent pamphlet called *The Court of Protection* and a booklet called *Enduring Powers of Attorney*. The latter explains clearly the procedure for making and registering Enduring Powers of Attorney. Both are free. The Public Trust Office is located at the same address as the Court of Protection (see above).

If you or your parent does not already have a solicitor and one has not been recommended by anyone, it is possible to contact The Law Society for their help. They can provide a list of names of solicitors in your area.

The Law Society
113 Chancery Lane
London WC2A 1PL
Tel: 071–242 1222

Further Reading
Age Concern England (address page 48) produces a factsheet (No 22), *Legal Arrangements for Managing Financial Affairs.*

As Scottish law differs in some respects, readers living in Scotland should contact Age Concern Scotland (address page 48) for factsheet No 22, available free on receipt of a 9-inch x 6-inch sae.

THE WILL

Most family lawyers will advise: 'There is only one way to make sure that your money is distributed in the way that you want after you die and that is to make a Will'.

A will is a formal expression of how the testator (the person making the will) wishes his or her property to be divided up when he or she dies. A little time spent in the preparation of a will to make intentions clear can result in a significant saving in time, hardship and money for the beneficiaries. Few actions can produce greater benefit for so little cost and effort, even though more than two thirds of adults have not yet made out a will. Cost should never be a barrier to drawing up a will; lawyers make far more money from unravelling both badly drawn up wills or those situations when no will has been prepared at all, than they do in drawing them up professionally in the first place.

The Law Society commissioned research that found various reasons why so few people make a will. Some people have never thought or have not wanted to think about it, others have not got around to it and many simply assume that their partner will automatically inherit everything. One in 10 did not want to think about dying, or believed that making a will was inviting premature death.

Although most children might feel reluctant about suggesting that their parents make a will, many old people feel much easier in their minds to know that their affairs are settled and that their assets and property are being distributed according to their wishes. This is discussed further in Chapter 12.

If a will is not made and a person dies intestate, the estate (the net personal assets of the deceased) will be divided by strict rules of law. This can cause difficulty for even the smallest estate, resulting in confusion, unnecessary cost and possible loss of capital and income for the beneficiaries.

Confusion is caused by the fact that agreement has to be reached over who should administer the estate; complications are caused by the need to divide the estate under the intestacy rules. Inheritance tax may end up being paid unnecessarily, as well as the assets being distributed in a way that would not necessarily have been approved of by the deceased.

For instance, if the deceased was married with children, under the intestacy rules the surviving spouse will receive only £75,000 plus the personal and household effects. The remainder is divided equally—half to the children and the balance held in trust. The surviving spouse only has a life interest in the amount held in Trust; he or she is able to receive an income but not to have access to the capital.

Once the decision has been made to make a will, it is essential for the person preparing it to receive legal advice. It is possible for a lay person to prepare a will him- or herself but this is not recommended. A solicitor will charge a fee (that should be negotiated in advance) and can advise on the best ways of structuring the will, taking into account numerous possibilities and provisions that would not necessarily be apparent to the lay person, in order to make the best provisions for the family and, if applicable, planning for inheritance tax.

Once a will is drawn up, for it to be valid under UK law it must be signed in front of two witnesses. The witnesses need not, and probably will not, read the contents of the will, but must sign the document themselves to evidence that it has been signed in front of them. They should observe the other's signature. Neither witness should be a beneficiary under the terms of the will.

An important part of the will is to ensure that there are correct executors to carry out the terms of the will and manage the estate. It is better to have two executors rather than one. Often a professional is appointed to handle the complex matters and inheritance tax, and a member of the family is appointed to ensure that the duties are discharged promptly and efficiently. Banks, accountants and solicitors all have specialist executor departments; all will charge for the service provided, with banks in particular being the most expensive, charging around 5 per cent of the value of the estate. It will normally be cheaper to use a provincial firm rather than one of the main London firms; however, cost should be measured against the quality of service to be provided.

In all cases permission should be sought from the persons appointed as executors under the terms of the will, as no one is bound to act as an executor.

Preparing a will correctly can secure significant tax savings; therefore a regular review is important to take the fullest advantage of changing legislation. Changes can be made to a will at any time by adding a supplementary *codicil* to the original will. The codicil must be signed and witnessed in the same way as the original will, although not necessarily by the same witnesses. *The original will must never be altered by way of insertion or deletion.* A will may also be revoked by making a new will, which must specify that it revokes all previous wills and codicils. A will may also be invalidated by marriage or remarriage, unless it has been prepared in anticipation of the event.

Another method by which the fullest advantage may be taken of all available tax reliefs is to leave the executors the discretion to override dispositions in the will. This can be done by providing the executors with restricted powers that enable them to change conditions of the will solely to avoid unnecessary taxation. These imposed restrictions on the discretion of the executor can be included in the will in such a way as to include or exclude as much as the testator wishes. It is normal to include restrictions to prevent the executor from having control over the primary distribution of the estate.

Once a will is made it should be lodged with a bank or lawyer. A copy, also stating where the original is kept, should always be filed with the testator's personal papers.

In any situation where explanations are needed about official documents or help or general advice are needed on any legal or administrative matter, contact the local Citizens Advice Bureau. They will also advise on local solicitors who could help.

The Will Registry
357–361 Lewisham High Street
London SE13 6NZ
Tel: 0303 248644

The Will Registry offers to prepare a single will for as little as £24.95. It will store wills for £14.95 per year.

Further Reading
Factsheet No 7 *Making Your Will*, Age Concern England (address page 48), free if an sae is sent with each request.

Age Concern also publish a leaflet, *Instructions for My Next of Kin and Executors upon my Death* (25p) which can be left in a convenient place to advise the family where to find the will and other important documents.

Don't Leave Your Money to Chance (Money Management Council, address page 124), free with sae.

Your Guide to Making a Will (Help the Aged, address page 49).

Wills and Probate (Consumer's Association, Castlemead, Gascoyne Way, Hertford SG14 1LH), £9.95

Written for the lay person, this includes excellent advice on the preparation of a will.

Inheritance Tax Planning—Leaving it to Your Family (KPMG Peat Marwick, 1 Puddle Dock, London EC4V 3PD), free.

DEBT

Although this is not strictly a legal issue, debt has become a major problem in recent years. The easy credit and boom years of the 1980s have combined to create a situation during the early 1990s in which many elderly people are facing severe financial hardship, often for the first time in their lives. The hardships may be a result of overcommitment, of unexpected unemployment or disability, or merely of the inflation of the 1970s and 1980s eating away at the fixed income that makes up the pension of many retired persons.

Excessive debt invariably generates severe stress and worry. Worse still, the situation will generally snowball unless properly managed and contained. If your parent or relative is in this situation, it is essential to discuss the problem and look at the various ways in which it might be alleviated. The Social Fund (see Chapter 6) can provide a small amount of assistance (never more than £1000), but is primarily aimed at providing loans for items that are difficult to budget for. This is generally inadequate except for the most desperate and needy cases.

The Citizens Advice Bureau or a Money Advice Centre, if there is one in the local area, will provide further advice. If necessary, free advice can also be obtained from a legal aid solicitor.

Other organisations committed to helping people in debt are:

Money Education, operating as
Money Management Council
PO Box 77
Hertford
Herts SG14 2HW
Tel: 0992 503448

Money Education is an independent impartial charity that promotes education in and better understanding of personal and family finance. The Council does *not* offer an individual advice service but it does produce a series of factsheets that are circulated to help/advisory agencies and direct to members of the public. This material is addressed primarily at people who are financially inexperienced.

Leaflets are available free from the above address, but people are asked to send an A4-sized sae.

Factsheets:
No 1 *You and Your Money (A General Introduction)*
No 3 *Where Can I Get Financial Advice?*
No 7 *Personal Budgeting*

National Debtline
The Birmingham Settlement
318 Summer Lane
Birmingham B19 3RL
Tel: 021–359 8501

National Debtline offers confidential and independent telephone advice to callers in England and Wales on all aspects of debt. The aim is to enable callers to deal with their debts with the assistance of a self-help pack, which is sent to individuals free of charge. They also provide booklets that are free to people in debt (for professionals and advisers there is a £2.50 fee):

Dealing with Your Debts—For
People with Mortgages
Dealing with Your Debts—For
People Who Pay Rent

Opening hours are 10 a.m. to 4 p.m. Monday and Thursday, 3 p.m. to 7 p.m. Tuesday and Wednesday. There is a 24-hour answering machine.

Further Reading
Debt: A Survival Guide
Creditwise
Both are free booklets published by the Office of Fair Trading, Field House, 15–25 Bream's Buildings, London EC4A 1PR. The former encourages openness with creditors and sets out a six-part action plan on how to cope with debt.

TAXATION

The principle behind taxation is not affected whatever the age of the taxpayer. However, there are additional allowances available to older persons, and this combined with their need to maximise income means there are additional considerations to be borne in mind.

Income Tax

Income tax is calculated over a tax year which runs from 6 April to 5 April. In the tax year, every individual is allowed a certain amount of tax-free income, called *personal allowances*. The total taxable income received is calculated, the personal allowances are deducted and the remaining amount is the figure on which tax is calculated. The lowest rate of tax for the year 1993/4 is 20 per cent and the highest is 40 per cent.

The basic personal allowances are £3,445 per person. These increase to £4,200 for people over 65 and under 75, and to £4,370 for those of 75 and over—but only if the individual's income does not exceed £14,200 for the tax year. Additional allowances are available for married persons, blind persons and for widows in the year that their husbands die and in the following year assuming that the widows do not remarry during that period.

Most income is taxable, but there are notable exceptions. These are:

- certain types of Social Security Benefit. These include benefits paid for illness or disability, such as Attendance Allowance or War Pensions.
- certain types of investment income. These include income from National Savings, TESSAs, and Personal Equity Plans, although all are subject to certain regulations.
- prizes and winnings, which are all tax-free, including those from Premium Bonds.

Most types of investment income have tax deducted at source, meaning that the interest or dividend is paid after deducting tax at 25 per cent. A non-taxpayer may prefer to select investments that do not deduct tax at source. It is also possible to request a bank or building society to pay interest gross, but only to someone who is not a taxpayer. There is a special form (R85) for this purpose, which is obtainable from banks, building societies and tax offices. There are about five million retired people who can register to have their income paid gross from a bank. Many have not done so.

If tax is deducted at source, it is possible to reclaim it at the end of the year by filling in a tax form if you are a non-taxpayer or are only likely to pay tax at 20 per cent. The Inland Revenue estimates that four million retired people have not reclaimed tax that they are owed, amounting to about £800 million.

Retirement pensions are normally all taxable. An exception to this is the amount by which a pension awarded on retirement through disability caused by industrial injury or work-related illness exceeds the pension which would have been paid if retirement had been on ordinary ill-health grounds. This amount is not treated as taxable income.

Further help can be obtained at the local Tax Enquiry Centre, which is in the telephone book under Inland Revenue, or from the local Citizens Advice Bureau. For those living in London, free advice on tax is available from the charitable trust TaxAid.

TaxAid
Linburn House
342 Kilburn High Road
London NW6 2QL

Tel: 071–624 3768 from 9 a.m. to 11 p.m. on weekdays for an appointment.

If your tax affairs or those of your parent are quite complex, it might be necessary to seek the help of an accountant. The Institute of Chartered Accountants will provide a list of appropriate local members. Always ask an accountant for an indication of the fee, preferably in writing, before making a commitment.

The Institute of Chartered
Accountants
Moorgate Place
London EC2 2BJ
Tel: 071–920 8100

Further Reading
Age Concern factsheet No 15, *Income Tax and Older People* (available free from Age Concern England, address page 48).
   Check Your Tax 1993/4 (free factsheet from Help the Aged, address page 49).
   Which? Way to Save Tax (published annually by Consumers Association, Castlemead, Gascoyne Way, Hertford, SG14 1LH), £11.95.
   Widows' Benefits and Tax, Paul Lewis (Saga Publishing Ltd, The Saga Building, Middleburg Square, Folkestone, Kent CT20 1AZ), free to Saga club members.

Inheritance Tax
Inheritance Tax applies to the estate of the deceased at the time of his or her death, and to transfers from the estate within a certain time before death (currently seven years). The rules are quite complex, so it is worth taking expert advice if an estate is large. Further information can also be obtained from the local Tax Enquiry Office or Citizens Advice Bureau.

In its most simple form, the value of an estate in excess of £150,000 is subject to tax at 40 per cent. This rate is applicable for 1993/4. Any transfers made within seven years of death will be taxed at the rate prevailing at the time of death, subject to a reduction of up to 80 per cent for transfers made between six and seven years before death.

Lifetime transfers made more than seven years before death are free of tax. Certain gifts, including gifts into and out of some trusts, will be taxed at half the death rates.

No tax is charged on an estate passing to a UK-domiciled spouse, or on bequests to a UK-based charity.

The executor of an estate is responsible for paying tax before distributions are made to beneficiaries under the will. (For more information see Chapter 12).

Further Reading
Booklet IHT1, *Inheritance Tax* (Capital Taxes Office, Minford House, Rockley Road, London W14 0DF)
   Inheritance Tax and Capital Gains Tax, Paul Lewis (Saga Publishing Ltd, The Saga Building, Middleburg Square, Folkestone, Kent CT20 1AZ), free to Saga club members

chapter eight

SPECIAL EQUIPMENT FOR DAILY LIFE

Small Gadgets and More Sophisticated Equipment
to Make Life Easier for Older People

As people grow older, they may find that ordinary, routine tasks may not be so easy to manage. A vast range of equipment is available to help make these tasks easier, from small items such as electric tin openers and gardening tools to larger devices such as stair lifts and adjustable beds.

The range of equipment is enormous and by no means only for the very frail or disabled—there are plenty of devices for people who are just realising that certain activities are slightly harder to manage than they used to be.

EQUIPMENT IDEAS

There are literally hundreds of labour- or effort-saving gadgets. I list just a few of them below in order to illustrate the vast range that is available, some so simple, others more sophisticated. The local Social Services Department will advise on funding for adaptations to your or your parents' home, for example handrails for the bathroom and stairs. Many of the other kitchen gadgets, cutlery, gardening equipment and other goods are available from the shops or mail-order catalogues listed at the end of this chapter.

In the Kitchen
Among the helpful kitchen gadgets available are the following:

KITCHEN PREPARATION
- slicing guides for cutting bread, fruit or vegetables
- a special rubber grip for opening bottles and jars, or a conical rubber twisting slot for one-handed opening
- mesh baskets for boiling foods in the pan (no need to lift the heavy pan to drain)
- special potato peelers, tin openers and butter spreaders
- excellent designs for taps to make them easier to operate
- kettle and pan stabilisers
- a variety of tongs, grips and reachers

- a range of 'tippers' for pouring from cartons, bottles, kettles and teapots

- special stands for hot water bottles (to assist filling)
- easy-grip handles for electric plugs

EATING AND DRINKING
- beakers with holders, cups with spouts and high-sided plates for single-handed eating
- combination easy-grip cutlery

which acts as knife, fork and spoon in one
- non-slip mats and trays and trays for one-handed carrying

Stairlifts and Lifts

Installing a stairlift can be the difference between staying in one's own home or having to move house. The lift can be installed on straight or curved staircases and may have a swivel seat for easy access, or may even carry a person in a wheelchair.

Your parent or relative should seek expert advice from, say, the Social Services Department, and should check the manufacturer's safety on design, construction, installation, operation and maintenance against the relevant British Standards before committing him- or herself to any stairlift.

Stannah Stairlifts Ltd is the world's leading manufacturer of stairlifts. Both standing and seated models are available, in an attractive range of fabrics and colours, to suit straight, curved or even spiral staircases. All products are fully approved to relevant British Standards and are comprehensively guaranteed.

For further information about Stannah Stairlifts write or telephone for a free information pack.

Stannah Stairlifts Ltd
Dept 6807
Freepost
Andover
Hants SP10 3BR
Tel: 0800 715116

Brooks Stairlifts Ltd
Westminster Ind Est
Station Road
North Hykeham
Lincoln LN6 3QY
Tel: 0522 500288

Selflift Chair Co
Mahler House
130 Worcester Road
Droitwich Spa
Worcs WR9 8AN
Tel: 0905 778 116

Gimson Stairlifts
62 Boston Road
Leicester LE4 1AZ
Tel: 0800 622251

Beds and Chairs

Several companies make adjustable manual or electric beds which can be adapted to the needs of older people, either for better and more comfortable sleep or for people who are bedridden.

Adjustable beds can raise the feet, the knees or allow for sitting up to read, eat or work. Alternatively, back rests can be used for a more upright position—there is even one which resembles the top half of an armchair.

Theraposture is an established family company which makes electric adjustable beds and seat-lift chairs in its own, purpose-built factory. All its equipment enables elderly or infirm people to remain independent in their own homes. Beds can be adjusted up and down, and head and foot can be adjusted for lying and sitting upright. Automatic chairs can lift or sit someone down gently, or recline for a restful sleep. Theraposture can provide free, 'no obligation' home demonstrations and brochures.

Theraposture Ltd
Warminster Business Park
Bath Road
Warminster
Wilts BA12 8PE
Tel: 0985 847788

Additional equipment for the bedroom can make life easier: a lifting pole by the bed to facilitate getting in and out, 'over-bed' tables (on wheels), powered, inflatable mattress-raisers and a selection of commodes.

Chairs have been designed to perform a number of functions. They can gently lean forward to help your parent stand up or lower him or her into sitting position, or recline (with or without a footrest) for reading, resting or sleeping. Some even combine heat and massage treatment.

Cumfi Care Upholstery
77a Broadstone Road
Reddish
Stockport
Cheshire SK5 7AS

Adjustamatic Beds
2 Lumley Road
Horley
Surrey RH6 7RJ
Tel: 0293 783837

Back-Care (Chairs)
Victoria Road
Off Bradford Rd
Dewsbury
W. Yorks WF13 2AB
Tel: 0924 464809

Recliners Unlimited
20 Cowbridge Road
Pontyclun
Mid Glamorgan CF7 9EE
Tel: 0443 229119

Concern for Comfort
Abacus House
Manor Road
London W13 0AS
Tel: 081–810 9508

Parker Hilton Ltd
Parker Hilton House
Primrose Street
Tyldesley
Manchester M29 8BQ
Tel: 0942 891818

Everstyl Reclining Armchairs
91 South End
Croydon CR0 1BG
Tel: 081–760 5178

Renray Group Ltd
Road Five
Winsford Industrial Estate
Winsford
Cheshire CW7 3RB
Tel: 0606 593456

Relief of Pressure Sores
Pressure sores, or bed sores, caused by periods of immobility can be very painful and difficult to heal. A number of specially-designed beds can alleviate the problem and provide comfort; fleeces, cushions, pads and rings can also help considerably.

In the Bathroom
It is vital that the bathroom is both safe and hygienic. A simple handrail or grabrail can be installed to prevent slipping or falling; these are available in a number of shapes and sizes.

Baths with built-in seating are available, but it is also possible to adapt an existing bath with a number of bath stools or chairs, some of which have a lifting facility or a 'swivel' action for further ease and safety. Special shower seats are also available.

A number of items are available to facilitate personal care, such as long-handled bath brushes, combs and hairbrushes, and wall-mounted dispensers for toothpaste, creams, etc.

Many older people find that the lavatory seat is too low. Raised seats are available, some with a gentle rising action and some with back rests or arm supports.

Special support frames fit around the lavatory for assistance. A number of rails in different shapes and sizes can be installed.

Parker Bath Developments
Stem Lane
New Milton
Hants BH25 5NN
Tel: 0425 622287

Dolphin Special Needs Bathrooms
Bromwich Road
Worcester WR2 4BD
Tel: 0905 748500

Niagara Therapy (UK) Ltd
Dartel House
2 Lumley Road
Horley
Surrey
Tel: 0293 784414

Douglas Industrial Sales
Springhill Kennylans Road
Sonning Common
Reading RG4 9JT
Tel: 0734 724266

For special mixer valves to fit on taps to prevent scalding:

Appollo Baths
Appollo House
34 Church Road
Romsey
Hants SO51 8EY
Tel: 0703 667711

Ambrose Wilson plc
Ambron House
PO Box 123
Dale Street
Manchester M60 1UH
Tel: 061–236 9911

Aqua Therapy Limited
Grosvenor House
Grafton Street
Altringham
Cheshire WA14 1BR
Tel: 061–929 9191

Miscellaneous Helpful Tools

- key-turners that fit on to keys to provide a proper handle
- large numbered playing cards, card shufflers and card holders
- clear, flat magnifiers
- easy-grip pens
- needle threaders
- special stands for help putting on stockings or tights
- long-handled shoe horns
- handreachers, some with magnetic ends for picking up pins and needles, with or without counter-balancers
- electric plugs with handles for a better grip
- footrests and 'leg loungers'

Walking trolleys are ideal for people who are not so steady on their feet: they combine a walking frame with a tray or trolley to enable people to move things around the house.

Alternatively, a multi-purpose lifter such as the *Mangar Booster* can be used. It can lift up to 20 stone in weight and can be used to pick up and carry luggage or equipment, or help to transfer people from chair to bed, floor to chair, etc.

The Mangar Booster Multi-Purpose Lifter
Presteigne Industrial Estate
Presteigne
Powys
Mid Wales
Tel: 0544 267674

In the Garden

* kneeler seats
* long-handled weeders, trowels, forks, flower-pickers and pruners (in lightweight materials)

Gardeners with special needs can find a list of useful tools and equipment, as well as a problem-solving service, from:

The Society for Horticultural Therapy
Trunkwell Park
Beech Hill
Reading RG7 2AT
Tel: 0734 884844

HEARING EQUIPMENT

Before buying equipment through advertisements or shops do consult a doctor. NHS hearing aids are more effective and less obtrusive than they have ever been. If your parent does choose one of the many commercially available hearing aids, check its claims and take advice before purchase, and make sure it is covered by British Standard BS6083. (See also Chapter 2, page 34.)

For guidance, Sound Advantage is part of the Royal National Institute for Deaf People (RNID) and provides a one-stop shop for the special needs of the deaf and hard of hearing. It sells a wide range of assistive products that can help make life easier and more enjoyable. They include listening products to help people hear conversations in crowded rooms and public places, TV and radio devices, alerting products (including flashing lights for the telephone or doorbell, smoke detectors and alarm clocks), and special telephones including textphones. A variety of free factsheets and a full product guide are available from:

Sound Advantage
1 Metro Centre
Welbeck Way
Peterborough PE2 7UH
Tel: 0733 361199

For books, literature and information on hearing aids:

Breakthrough Deaf-Hearing Integration
Birmingham Centre
Charles W. Gillett Centre
998 Bristol Road
Selly Oak
Birmingham B29 6LE
Tel: 021–472 6447

Hidden Hearing Ltd
6 Clarendon Place
King Street
Maidstone
Kent ME14 1BR
Tel: 0622 691848

Telephones

The Chronically Sick and Disabled Persons Act 1970 gives local authorities a duty to provide a telephone for certain disabled people or help them to get a telephone. Each local authority will have its own guidelines on what it will provide—this may include installation (and sometimes rental) of special phones with signalling handsets for people with hearing difficulties and inductive couplers to eliminate background noise.

People on Income Support may be able to get a loan from the Social Fund (see page 112). For further advice and information contact the Social Services Department or DIEL (address below).

DIEL is the Advisory Committee on Telecommunications for Disabled and Elderly People and produces an information pack on telephone services for use by older or disabled people and their helpers. This includes information on installation and rental charges, billing services for visually impaired people, telephones for hard of hearing people and telephone systems for people with limited dexterity or mobility. Copies of the information pack are available from:

DIEL
Second Floor
Room 2/3
Export House
50 Ludgate Hill
London EC4M 7JJ
Tel: 071–634 8700

Typetalk is a new telephone relay service developed jointly by the RNID and BT. It is designed to give deaf, deafened, deaf-blind, hard of hearing and speech-impaired people access to a public telephone network which matches the quality of service currently enjoyed by hearing people. Calls are relayed to and from people using textphones throughout the UK to hearing people worldwide. Typetalk is open 24 hours a day, seven days a week, 365 days a year, and users pay virtually the same as a hearing person would for the same call had it been dialled direct. Users can claim a rebate from BT by telephoning their local office (telephone number on the telephone bill). Further information and free leaflets from:

Typetalk
Pauline Ashley House
Ravenside Retail Park
Speke Road
Liverpool L24 8QB
Tel: 051–494 1000
Text: 0800 500800

Age Concern England (address page 48) publishes a leaflet (No 28), *Help with Telephones*.

FOR THE BLIND AND PARTIALLY SIGHTED

For equipment, advice, literature and games:

Royal National Institute for the Blind (RNIB)
224 Great Portland Street
London W1N 6AA
Tel: 071–388 1266

FOOTWEAR

It may be difficult for older people to find footwear which is both comfortable and stylish in soft materials with wide fittings. They should not be tempted to wear a favourite pair of slippers all day as this can exacerbate foot problems. Several specialist mail-order companies make broad-fitting, quality leather footwear.

AJE Footfitters (home shopping)
3 Prospect Yard
Wakefield
W. Yorks WE1 1XW
Tel: 0924 371259

The London Shoe Clinic
2a East Mount Street
London E1 1BA
Tel: 071–790 1747

Wide Shoes of Welling
19 Bellegrove Road
Welling
Kent DA15 3PA

GENERAL EQUIPMENT DISTRIBUTORS

A great many of the items I have listed are available commercially but, if your parent or relative is disabled, the local Social Services Department may be able to assist. Your parent's doctor will have a list of equipment that may be prescribed or may be available from the Department of Health. Alternatively, your parent should talk to his or her district nurse, health visitor or social worker.

There are many organisations that distribute a range of equipment. The Disabled Living Centres Council is the national organisation of 35 independent Disabled Living Centres in the UK which provide assessment, advice and information on daily living. The majority of centres also have a large range of equipment on display; trained advisers are able to offer impartial advice and so help avoid costly mistakes. Equipment includes children's equipment, clothing and footwear, continence management, communication equipment and help with eating and drinking, hoists and lifting, mobility, personal care, seating and sleeping. For information on the nearest centre, contact:

The Disabled Living Centres Council
286 Camden Road
London N7 0BJ
Tel: 071–700 1707

The Disabled Living Foundation
380–384 Harrow Road
London W9 2HU
Tel: 071–289 6111
The Disabled Living Foundation (part of the DLCC) responds to over 30,000 letters and telephone calls a year about where people can obtain equipment, footwear and clothing and on all aspects of independent living. It has a permanent exhibition of equipment and aids, from small gadgets to wheelchairs, which can be seen by appointment in London.

The Northern Ireland Information Service for Disabled People
2 Annadale Avenue
Belfast BT7 3JR
Tel: 0232 491011

Disability Scotland Information Service
5 Shandwick Place
Edinburgh EH2 4RG
Tel: 031–229 8632

Wales Council for the Disabled (Cyngor Cymru I'r Anabl)
Llys Ifor
Crescent Road
Caerphilly
Mid Glamorgan CF8 1XL
Tel: 0222 887325

Designed for Living
Arthritis Care
18 Stephenson Way
London NW1 2HD
Tel: 071–916 1500

The Disability Information Trust
Mary Marlborough Lodge
Nuffield Orthopaedic Centre
Headington
Oxford OX3 7LD
Tel: 0865 227591/2
The Disability Information Trust is a registered charity, supported by the Department of Health, whose main activity is to assess and test a whole range of disability equipment and publish the results in its series of books *Equipment for Disabled People*. Full details of all products are included along with descriptive comments, photographs, specifications, manufacturers and prices. In addition, much advice is offered in the form of points to consider before any purchase is

made. Most aspects of daily living are included and the series comprises 14 titles, from outdoor transport to home management. A free descriptive leaflet is available on request.

REMAP GB
Hazeldene
Ightham
Sevenoaks
Kent TN15 9AD
Tel: 0732 883818
REMAP can design, manufacture and supply aids and equipment free of charge for people with disabilities whose problems cannot be solved with standard commercial equipment. This is made possible by volunteers all over the country who contribute their time and skills. Leaflets are available free of charge.

The British Red Cross Society
9 Grosvenor Crescent
London SW1X 7EJ
Tel: 071–235 5454
The Red Cross has 1000 depots across the UK carrying stocks of items for short-term loan. Charges are modest and may be waived in cases of hardship. In addition, its range of services includes therapeutic beauty care, mobility aids, medical loans, escort and transport services, first-aid duties and training, a home-from-hospital scheme and holidays.

HOUSEHOLD AND GENERAL EQUIPMENT

Home and Comfort
PO Box 25
Wellesbourne
Warwick CV35 9TY
Tel: 0789 470055
Mail-order goods including bath handles, hearing amplifiers, extending shoe trees, etc.

Special Equipment and Aids For Living
Ddol Hir
Glyn Ceirlog
Clwyd LL20 7NP
Tel: 0691 718331

CC Products (Dept DT4)
152 Markham Road
Charminster
Bournemouth BH9 1JE
Tel: 0202 522260
Manufacturers of a 'portaloo' for long journeys.

Homecraft Supplies Ltd
Farnham Trading Estate
Farnham
Surrey GU9 9NN
Tel: 0252 714182
Homecraft produces a catalogue of special products for older people, from household and kitchen items to ramps and wheelchairs.

Keep Able
Fleming Close
Park Farm
Wellingborough
Northants NN8 6UF (Catalogue only, shops in London and W. Midlands)
Tel: 0933 679426
Large range of small items and larger goods and equipment for the house and garden, available from shops or by catalogue.

Chester-Care
Low Moor Estate
Kirkby in Ashfield
Notts NG17 7JZ
Tel: 0623 757955
Catalogue of small and larger household items for independent life at home.

Infratech
PO Box 216
Luton
Beds LU3 1QX
Tel: 0582 455239
Products to enhance the volume of the television for the hearing impaired.

Nanas and Papas Ltd
21 Francis Street
Leicester LE2 2BE
Tel: 0533 705671
Mail-order goods and clothes.

The Special Collection
J. D. Williams
53 Dale Street
Manchester M60 6ES
Tel: 061-228 0626
Comfortable, easy to wear mail-order clothes.

Dressense
49–67 Northcote Road
Bournemouth BH1 4SQ
Tel: 0202 298511
Mail-order clothes.

Further Reading
Directory of Aids for Disabled and Elderly People, Ann Darnbrough and Derek Kinrade (Woodhead-Faulkner, 1986), £14.95

chapter nine

KEEPING SAFE

*Home Protection, Basic Safety Guidelines
and Where to Turn for Help*

IT IS IMPORTANT that older people know that their homes and they themselves are safe at all times—safe from accidents in the home or from criminal acts. Accidents do happen but most can be avoided by taking precautions. Crime statistics do make disturbing reading but, in fact, figures show that elderly people are less likely to be attacked or robbed than any other age group. By taking reasonable precautions and avoiding danger there is no reason why older people should not live their lives with complete confidence and security.

WHO CAN HELP?

Help the Aged offer the most comprehensive help in the form of advice, literature and equipment about the risks and prevention of fire, burglary and break-ins and accidents in the home. Further details are given in this chapter and for leaflets (detailed below) send sae:
Security in Your Home
Safety In Your Home
Be Sure Who's At The Door
Fire

Help the Aged
St James Walk
London EC1R 0BE
Tel: 071–253 0253
Seniorline (free): 0800 289404 (10 a.m.
to 4 p.m.)
Advice Line: 071–250 3399

Royal Society for Prevention of Accidents (ROSPA)
Cannon House
The Priory, Queensway
Birmingham B4 6BS
Tel: 021–200 2461
The ROSPA publishes two leaflets:
RSDR167, *Older and Wiser—Road
    Safety for Older People*, £1.90
HS55, *Home Safety Factsheet—
    Safety of Older People*, £1.90

HELP IN AN EMERGENCY

Community alarms are a boon to people living on their own and enable them to call for help even if they cannot reach a telephone. All that is needed is a telephone line and an electric 13-amp power point. A special button on the telephone or on a pendant will alert control centre staff who can speak to the user (even if he or she cannot reach the telephone) and send whatever help is necessary. These alarms are not just for use in emergency: staff at the control centre can also provide friendly advice and assistance.

Help the Aged runs a national alarms scheme throughout the UK. Advice can be given on whether the local authority has an alarm scheme, what it will cost and whom to contact. If a suitable scheme is not available locally, the charity's aim is to obtain an alarm for older people who could benefit from one. In addition, Help the Aged can advise on which housing associations and commercial firms offer alarm systems.

Community Alarms Department
Help the Aged
St James Walk
London EC1R 0BE
Tel: 0800 289 404

Age Concern recommends the *ComCare Messenger*, a monitoring service which incorporates an emergency button, visual ringing telephone, remote control pendant or clip, high-speed dialling, adjustable volume and ring tone, hands-free operation and activity monitor which will check up on your parent if he or she does not use the phone during the pre-arranged period of your choice. For costs and further information contact Age Concern/ComCare free on 0800 300123.

Watchbase Communications operates a similar scheme.

Watchbase Communications
George House
121 High Street
Henley in Arden
Warwicks B95 5AU
Tel: 0564 794044

SECURITY IN THE HOME

Most break-ins are not the work of professional burglars. Many are carried out by opportunists: petty thieves who see an open window or insecure door.

Remind older people that if they are going out even for a few moments they should check that all doors and windows are securely locked. If they are going away on holiday they must be sure to cancel all deliveries—milk on the doorstep for a few days is a true give-away. They should also ask neighbours to keep an eye on their home and report anything suspicious.

Garden tools should be locked away—a ladder can be very useful for the opportunistic burglar. And remind older relatives and friends not to display their home address on the outside of their luggage—why advertise a departure to burglars who are lurking at the airport or ferry terminal? Companies such as Homesitters (address page 93) can offer security and peace of mind to holidaymakers.

Closed and locked windows are an effective deterrent to burglars—they will rarely break a window and risk the noise or danger of cuts. Keys should be removed from locked windows and kept out of sight and reach.

A front door should be made of solid wood, with a strong frame, a good lock and at least one dead lock, a door viewer and a security chain. Back and side doors are equally vulnerable.

Extra security in the form of intruder alarms and exterior lighting can help fight crime and make the house more secure. The local Crime Prevention Officer (at local police stations) should be able to discuss alternatives and give advice.

Marking Possessions

Valuables are more likely to be found by the police if a record is kept of serial numbers and property is marked with the owner's postcode. This can be done by etching, die-stamping or using a security marker which can only be read under an ultra-violet light. Local Crime Prevention Officers or Neighbourhood Watch Groups can give details of where to get this marking equipment. They will also advise where a window sticker can be obtained to warn thieves that property is marked. In addition, a full list of valuable items with descriptions and colour photographs can greatly assist in returning stolen property.

A 40-page handbook entitled *Practical Ways to Crack Crime* and its shorter version *The Family Guide* are useful Home Office publications available free of charge in a range of different languages. Telephone 081–569 7000 (24 hrs) to request copies.

Neighbourhood Watch schemes are self-help groups which work in partnership with the police. They aim to prevent crime and are able to offer valuable neighbourly help and advice. Ask the local Crime Prevention Officer if there is a scheme locally and, if not, why not help to set one up?

IF THE HOUSE IS BURGLED...
• Do not touch anything.
• Contact the police straight away.

Victim Support Schemes

If your or your parent's home is broken into or he or she is robbed on the street it can be an extremely upsetting experience. Victim Support Schemes can help and advise people who have suffered such experiences. They can provide support and understanding to people who need to get over the shock and regain their self-confidence. Ask the local police station for the nearest branch or contact:

The National Association of Victim Support Schemes
39 Brixton Road
London SW9 6DZ
Tel: 071–735 9166

Victim Support Scotland
14 Frederick Street
Edinburgh EH2 2HB
Tel: 031–225 7779/8233

Crime Concern
David Murray John Building
Brunel Centre
Swindon
Wilts SN1 1LY
Tel: 0793 514596
Crime Concern is a national organisation responsible for supporting and developing crime prevention activity. It can offer advice on many different aspects of crime prevention.

The Criminal Injuries Compensation Board
200 West Regent Street
Glasgow G2 4SW
Tel: 041–221 0945
Anyone who has been injured as a direct result of a crime may be eligible for compensation. *A Guide to The Criminal Injuries Compensation Scheme* sets out who can apply and what injuries qualify. Victims may need the services of a solicitor or

adviser, but the Board will not cover the cost of this.

SOS Talisman
TALMAN Ltd
Gray's Inn Corner
Ley Street
Ilford
Essex IG2 7RQ
Tel: 081–554 5579
Personal alarms.

Aid Call plc
363 Fulham Road
London SW10 9BR
Tel: 071–352 2822
Medical/panic personal alarm with transmitter to central monitoring centre.

Response Electronics plc
Unit 1
First Quarter
Longmead Industrial Estate
Blenheim Road
Epsom
Surrey KT19 9QN
Tel: 0372 744330
Burglar alarms.

Securador
125 Oxford Road
Windsor SL4 5DX
Tel: 0753 850549
Security doors.

Someone at the Door?

It makes sense to be cautious when the doorbell goes and your parents or older relatives should not be embarrassed about refusing to let someone in—it is *their* home. They should use the door viewer to see who it is and, if they do not know them, they should put on the chain before opening the door. If the caller has a good reason for being there, he or she will not mind being asked for an identification card.

If they are still not happy, they should ask for the name and the telephone number of the organisation the caller claims to represent, keep the chain on the door and telephone the organisation. If they do not have a telephone, they can just send the caller away. They can always ask him or her to return when they have a friend or neighbour there. If they are still suspicious they should dial 999 and ask for the police.

STAYING SAFE AND ACTIVE

It is important that older people are safe from everyday accidents, most of which can be prevented. A few important practical steps can avoid the most common domestic accidents:

- Even in familiar surroundings, good lighting can help prevent a fall, particularly on the stairs.
- If climbing the stairs is difficult, handrails on both sides can help.
- Sturdy shoes with rubberised soles and non-slip heels can help with stability.
- Lifting heavy objects or bags should be avoided—ask for help.
- Rearranging the furniture so that everyone can move about freely and without bumping into things is always a good idea.
- No trailing flexes or rucked up carpets should be left to trip up on.

The Royal Society for the Prevention of Accidents (ROSPA) publish leaflets and information about safety in the home (address page 159).

TAKING MEDICATION

Some points to remember when advising older people:

- Keep all medicines out of reach of any young children who may visit.
- Make sure they understand the instructions on the label and ask their pharmacist if they are in any doubt. The right amount at the right time will help them get better: anything else may be harmful.
- Ask the pharmacist about pill dispensers as these can help to organise daily requirements.
- Some caps on bottles are child-proof—and often fairly adultproof, too! The pharmacist can help if they have problems.
- Return unused medicines to the pharmacist.

FIRE

One of the most important investments anyone can make in the home is a smoke alarm. Even a small fire can be destructive and traumatic. A smoke alarm can detect the first whiff of smoke and avoid a great deal of damage.

Basic smoke alarms can be purchased at comparatively low prices. Choose one bearing the British Standard Number BS5446 and the Kite Mark. Smoke alarms can be fitted in any room where a fire might start (but not in the kitchen or bathroom as steam or ordinary cooking fumes could trigger the alarm) and at the bottom of each staircase. B & Q stores sell smoke alarms and offer a 10 per cent discount to members of the B & Q over-60s club (see page 177 for details). The instructions will advise on the best site for an alarm. The alarm will indicate when its batteries need to be changed.

British Gas will carry out a free gas safety check on gas appliances if:

- your parent or relative is over 60 years of age and lives alone or with someone who also qualifies
- he or she is a registered disabled person of any age and lives alone or with someone who also qualifies
- he or she receives a state disability benefit and lives alone or with someone who also qualifies

The check will consist of a basic examination and includes any necessary adjustments and materials up to a cost of £2.50 plus VAT. If as a result of the check any additional work needs to be done it will have to be paid for, so ask for an estimate first. If your parent receives Income Support ask at the local Department of Social Security office to see if your parent is entitled to any financial assistance, before ordering the work to be done.

A free booklet, *Advice for Older People*, gives information about the free gas safety check and special adapters which can be fitted free of charge to some gas fires and cookers to make the controls easier to use. Also, *Help Yourself to Gas Safety* is available free of charge from the local British Gas Showroom (the telephone number is in the telephone book under 'Gas').

Smokers

Smokers should use plenty of deep ashtrays and be sure to put them in places where they cannot be knocked over. Remind older relatives to be sure to stub out their cigarette properly, particularly before emptying the ashtray into a bin, and to check they have not left a burning cigarette in an ashtray before going out or going to bed. They should appreciate the great dangers of smoking in bed.

In the Kitchen

When cooking with fats and oils due care must be taken never to leave pans unattended and to lower the temperature if they start spitting. If a frying or chip pan catches fire, *never* pour water on it. Turn off the heat and smother the flames with the pan lid or a damp cloth or blanket and leave it to cool for at least half an hour. It is best to call the fire brigade even if the fire appears to be out. If you are thinking of buying your parents a fire blanket, make sure you choose one bearing the British Standard number BS6575.

Heaters

Ensure heaters are used away from bed clothes, furniture or curtains and that they are not in a position where they could be knocked over. Sitting too close to a heater should always be avoided as clothes could catch fire. Paraffin heaters should always be filled out of doors and never filled or moved when alight.

Electricity

All electrical equipment should be checked regularly by a competent electrician for safety. A list of approved contractors can be found at most Electricity Board shops or local reference libraries. Fuses should be checked for the correct rating and flexes checked to make sure that they are not too long or worn.

Avoid placing a flex under carpeting, as this damages the flex. Do not overload power points by using multiple adaptors. If any piece of electrical equipment cuts out continually or gives off a strange smell, or if the plug feels warm, switch it off immediately and have it checked.

IN CASE OF FIRE

- Keep all internal doors closed.
- See that everyone gets out of the house.
- Call the fire brigade by dialling 999 from a neighbour's house.
- Do not attempt to re-enter the house.

IF UNABLE TO GET OUT OF THE HOUSE

- Go to a room unaffected by the fire, preferably one facing the street.
- Close the door behind you.
- Block the foot of the door with bedclothes, cushions, etc.
- Open the window and shout or wave to attract attention.
- Get somebody to call the fire brigade and await their arrival.

Further Reading
Dispersed Alarm Systems in the UK—A Listing of Central Controls and Appraisal of Current Issues, Malcolm J. Fisk (compiler) (The Planning Exchange 1990), £18

chapter ten

MOBILITY AND GETTING AROUND

Transport Schemes and Special Vehicles to Help Older People Stay Mobile

ONE OF THE WAYS of maintaining independence for as long as possible is to keep fit and mobile, and mobility around the home is as important as being able to get out and about.

Walking sticks and frames, in a wide variety designs and grips, are available by prescription or commercially. Whichever your parent or relative decides on, they should always check it bears the British Standards Kite Mark. Stairlifts, walking frames that double as trolleys for transporting things around the house or with seats or shopping baskets attached and other useful mobility aids are discussed in Chapter 8.

For further details on the provision of equipment, older people should first check to see what is available through their Social Services Department. Certain equipment is available on loan from the British Red Cross Society (address page 58) or for sale from The Disabled Living Centres Council (address page 58). For information about white sticks for people with loss of sight contact the RNIB (address page 156).

People who are unable to walk or cannot walk more than a short distance, and either drive a car or are driven by someone else, can ask their local Social Services Department (see telephone book under Social Services for the local council or borough) about the national Orange Badge Scheme. Many places have parking spaces specially reserved for cars displaying the orange badge on the windscreen; bearers may also stop for a limited time in places where parking is not normally allowed. Further details are also available in a leaflet from:

The Disability Unit
Room S10/21
Department of Transport
2 Marsham Street
London SW1P 3EB
Tel: 071–276 5257 or 5252

BUS TRAVEL

Fare concessions are available on buses; these vary from one local authority to another. In some, travel is free at certain times or available at reduced rates for women over 60 and men over 65. For further information on concessionary rates and bus passes look for information at the local library, Citizens Advice Bureau or contact the local Age Concern group (address page 48).

RAIL TRAVEL

People over 60 are entitled to a Senior Railcard which offers one third off the price of leisure travel for a year from the date of purchase. Railcards may be bought for £16 from British Rail stations or selected travel agents. To apply people will need to take some form of proof of age such as a passport, NHS Medical card, birth certificate or current Senior Railcard.

A Senior Railcard entitles people to ⅓ off the price of:

- Savers and Supersavers
- Network AwayBreaks
- Cheap Day Singles and Returns
- Standard Single and Open Returns
- First-Class Single and Open Returns
- First-Class and Standard Day
- Singles[1]
- First-Class and Standard Day Returns[1]
- All zones One Day Travelcards subject to minimum fare[2]
- Rail Rovers[3]

Discounts are also available to holders on some ferry services.

Please check for full details at local stations as there may be certain ticket, route, train and time restrictions applicable.

A Senior Railcard does *not* give a discount on:

- Special excursions and Charters (i.e. those not listed in public timetables)
- Railair Coach Links
- Boat trains between London
- (Victoria) and Channel ports, or between London (Waterloo) and Southampton Docks
- Any non-BR services other than those already mentioned.

Leisure First

Leisure First offers off-peak First-Class travel at half the usual First-Class fare. It is be available in limited numbers on most InterCity trains throughout the

1 These discounts are not available within the Network South East area on peak morning services on Monday to Friday (not including Bank Holidays). Please enquire at the local station for details.
2 No discount available on Network South East Rail Rovers.
3 No discounts on 1–2 zone, 1–4 zone and 2–6 zone One Day Travelcards.

week, with the exception of those running at peak business times.

To qualify for Leisure First people must spend a Saturday night away and reserve seats no later than 16.00 the day before travel. Further details and conditions are available in the Leisure First leaflet available from BR.

Rail Europe Senior Card

With a Senior Railcard people can buy a Rail Europe Senior Card for just £5. This offers savings on rail and sea travel to 19 European Countries.

The Rail Europe Senior Card and details of fares to individual destinations are available at main British Rail stations, British Rail International appointed Travel Agents or from:

The International Rail Centre
Victoria Station
London SW1V 1JY
Tel: 071–834 2345#

TRIPSCOPE

Tripscope provides a national telephone-based information service on transport and travel for elderly and disabled people. It can provide information on travel options by public transport and more specialised services for those planning specific journeys both in the UK and overseas. They will also offer assistance and information about related matters such as accessible lavatories and wheelchair hire, and will deal with enquiries by telephone, letter or tape.

The service is free both to individual disabled or elderly people and professionals and organisations working with them. Tripscope is not a travel agency and cannot make bookings. For further information contact:

Jim or Adrian
The Courtyard
Evelyn Road
London W4 5JL
Tel: 081–994 9294
UK (except the southwest) and International.

John
Pamwell House
160 Pennywell Road
Bristol BS5 OTX
Tel: 0272 414094
Southwest.

VOLUNTARY AND COMMUNITY TRANSPORT SCHEMES

Further information on local mobility and voluntary and community transport services may be obtained from the Department of Transport Disability Unit at:

The Disability Unit
Room S10/21
Department of Transport
2 Marsham Street
London SW1P 3EB
Tel: 071–276 5252/5257 or 4973

DIAL-A-RIDE AND TAXICARD

DaRT—Dial-a-Ride and Taxicard Users—represents over 15,000 Londoners with disabilities who are unable to use public transport. DaRT carries out and publishes research on the two specialist transport services for people with disabilities, Dial-a-Ride and Taxicard, and works to persuade central and local government to recognise the need for increased funding for both services. DaRT also carries out research and promotes fully accessible mainstream public transport—buses, tubes and trains.

Members of Dial-a-Ride and Taxicard can join DaRT for an annual voluntary membership fee of £2 (£1 if on a low income) and receive regular information which keeps them up to date on all transport issues affecting people with disabilities. DaRT is funded by the London Borough Grants Committee. For free leaflets on the service, and others such as:
Accessible Buses
How to Get Disabled People Moving in London
Transport in European Capitals
   contact:

DaRT
St Margaret's
25 Leighton Road
London NW5 2QD
Tel: 071–482 2325

Dial-a-Ride

Dial-a-Ride is a door-to-door transport service for people who are unable to use public transport. It is available to people of any age and any disability. Dial-a-Ride mini-buses are specially designed. All of them can carry wheelchair users and Dial-a-Ride drivers will help passengers on and off the bus and see them safely to their doors.

Passengers pay their own fare—about the same as an ordinary bus—and may travel alone or accompanied to go shopping, to visit friends, etc. Dial-a-Ride cannot take people to hospital appointments as this service should be provided by the non-emergency ambulance service.

The Dial-a-Ride service runs seven days a week throughout the year and operates throughout the Greater London area. Anyone wishing to join the service should contact DaRT for the local Dial-a-Ride address.

Taxicard

The Taxicard Scheme allows people with disabilities who are unable to use mainstream public transport to use licensed London cabs at a reduced rate. Taxicard holders can book a cab for any purpose at any time and can travel anywhere in the Greater London area.

Taxicard is operated and funded in most London boroughs and membership of the scheme is usually free. In most boroughs there are restrictions to the number of trips a Taxicard holder can make.

In most boroughs Taxicard users can make a journey costing up to £10.60 on the taximeter for a flat fee of £1.40. Any amount over the £10.60 limit must be paid in full. To join the London-wide scheme contact:

LATU (The London Accessible Transport Unit)
Britannia House
1–11 Glenthorpe Road
London W6 0LF
Tel: 081–748 7272

The British Red Cross Society (address page 58) provides volunteers and escorts to enable housebound and handicapped people to make journeys.

Hertz Rent-a-Car
Head Office
1272 London Road
London SW16 4DQ
Tel: 081–679 1799
Hertz Rent-a-Car is purported to be the only car hire firm which is prepared to rent cars to individuals over 74 years of age.

The Disabled Drivers' Association
Ashwellthorpe
Norwich, NR16 1EX
Tel: 050 841 449
The Disabled Drivers' Association promotes independence through mobility for the disabled and will help with legal problems, information and social groups.

The Chalfont Line
4 Medway Parade
Perivale
Middlesex UB6 8HA
Tel: 081–997 3799
The Chalfont Line provides transport (and holidays) for disabled and elderly people.

AIR TRAVEL

Most airlines are extremely helpful to anyone with a disability or those who cannot manage the enormous distances that they may have to cover between the terminal and the aircraft. If they are informed well in advance that a passenger may need assistance, they may be able to arrange transport from check-in to the aircraft and priority seating. They should also be informed if a passenger will be taking a wheelchair, walking frame or other aid.

LOW-SPEED VEHICLES

A number of different low-speed, battery-powered vehicles are on the market which do not require a driving licence. Many have optional hoods, shopping baskets and other accessories and may be driven on the pavement as they only travel at a few miles per hour. For further information contact the nearest Disabled Living Centre (address page 156) or RADAR (address page 58).

Anyone considering buying one of these vehicles should check the cost of maintenance, as replacement tyres, batteries and labour charges may be high. Brochures and 'test drives' should be free of charge.

Other suppliers include:

The Bedford Mobility Centre
Freepost 348
Watford
Herts WD2 8FP
Tel: 0234 266666

Genesis Mobility
Genesis House
Abbots Morton
Worcs WR7 4NA
Tel: 0386 792123

Ortho Kinetics UK Ltd
Freepost
Wedensfield
Wolverhampton WC13 3XA
Tel: 0902 866166

EEZEE-Rise
Body Therapy
72 Babbacombe Road
Torquay
Devon TQ1 3SW
Tel: 0803 322533

Electric Mobility Euro Ltd
Sea King Road
Lynx Trading Estate
Yeovil
Somerset BA20 2YS
Tel: 0935 22156

Further Reading
Directory of Aids for Disabled and Elderly People, Ann Darnbrough and Derek Kinrade (Woodhead-Faulkner, 1986), £14.95
Out and About: A Travel and Transport Guide, Richard Armitage and John Taylor (Age Concern, 1990), £6.95

c h a p t e r   e l e v e n

HOBBIES AND INTERESTS

Helping Your Parents Explore
Further Education, Volunteering and Other New Pursuits

FOR MANY PEOPLE, retirement offers opportunities to follow up new or favourite hobbies, interests and activities for which there may not have been time previously. There is such an exciting choice of activities, courses, sports and games on offer that it can make retirement into a new beginning.

In Chapter 2 I discussed the importance of keeping fit and of healthy exercise; in that chapter many forms of exercise and relaxation were examined. Local authorities arrange many sporting or leisure activities. It is worth checking at the local library to investigate the huge range of adult education courses which are offered—such as languages, painting, cooking or photography—and for details on facilities or classes at the nearest leisure centre. They should also have information on any local interest groups, sports clubs and other group arrangements.

NEW BEGINNINGS

The Dark Horse Venture
Kelton
Woodlands Road
Liverpool, L17 0AN
Tel: 051–729 0092
'The Dark Horse Venture—discovering the dark horse in you!'

One exciting development is The Dark Horse Venture, which is open to all over 55 and encourages them to take up new activities and discover hidden talents. To qualify, all they have to do is select an activity which they have never tried before and pursue it on a regular basis for a minimum of 12 months. During this time, they will receive guidance and advice from a chosen person with professional training or proven experience in that activity. Dark Horse Venture Certificates are awarded on satisfactory completion of the chosen activity.

Three different categories exist; almost any activity will fit into one of these:.

1. Giving and Sharing: being involved with and offering assistance to other people in the community. Practical help includes dog-walking, shopping, staffing hospi-

tal canteens, fundraising or qualifying in first-aid or life-saving techniques.
2. Learning and Doing: non-physical, individual or group hobbies. These might include acting, collecting, cooking, drawing, decorating, fishing, investing or singing.
3. Exploring and Exercising; undertaking travel, explorations or physical recreation. This might be bowling, swimming, rambling or travelling, to name just a few possibilities.

There is no limit to the number of single subject certificates that people can embark on and win. Those who have been awarded one certificate from each of the three categories can apply for the Gold Seal Certificate. For a general information pack and registration form, contact The Dark Horse Agency at the address given above.

Age Resource
Astral House
1268 London Road
London SW16 4ER
Tel: 081–679 2201
Age Resource was established by Age Concern England to ensure that knowledge, skills and experience gained during the first 50 or 60 years of life should be developed, diversified, utilised and enjoyed. It promotes a wide range of opportunities for involvement by older people and develops and expands contacts and co-operation with other organisations. In addition it makes awards to celebrate the achievements of older people in group activities.

Third Age Trust
1 Stockwell Green
London SW9 9JF
Tel: 071–737 2541
Forms over-55s groups to study or participate in leisure activities.

The Scottish Retirement Council
204 Bath Street
Glasgow G2 4HL
Tel: 041–332 9427
The Scottish Retirement Council promotes education for retired people and runs a number of craft and hobby centres.

REACH
89 Southwark Street
London SE1 0HX
Tel: 071–928 0452
REACH finds part-time expenses-only jobs for retired or redundant business- or other professional men and women who want to use their skills to help charitable organisations, depending on their experience and availability. Regional 'matchers', themselves retired professional people, send anyone interested a selection of jobs to consider.

The New Horizons Trust
Paramount House
290–292 Brighton Road
S. Croydon
Surrey CR2 6AG
Tel: 081–666 0201
The New Horizons Trust utilises the skills and experience of the recently retired in projects of benefit to the community in general.

VOLUNTEERING

A vast number of organisations survive on the work of volunteers. Help is always gratefully received, will sometimes pay moderate expenses, will enable volunteers to choose the amount of hours they work and may require some training. Here are just a few—more are listed on page 58:

Age Concern England
(address page 48)

Help the Aged
(address page 49)

Community Service Volunteers
237 Pentonville Road
London N1 9NG
Tel: 071–278 6601

British Trust for Conservation Volunteers
36 St Mary's Street
Wallingford
Oxon OX10 0EU
Tel: 0491 839766

Voluntary Service Overseas
317 Putney Bridge Road
London SW15 2PG
Tel: 081–780 2266

National Association of Leagues of Hospital Friends
Second Floor
Fairfax House
Colchester
Essex CO1 1RJ
Tel: 0206 761227

FURTHER EDUCATION

The Council for the Accreditation of Correspondence Colleges is a registered charity which accredits organisations offering home-study courses. It aims to promote education and training and to raise standards of tuition in distance education. Some 200 courses at 41 colleges are currently listed in an information leaflet which is available free of charge from:

Council for the Accreditation of Correspondence Colleges
27 Marylebone Road
London NW1 5JS
Tel: 071–935 5391

Education Resources for Older People
The City Lit
Bolt Court
Fleet Street
London EC4A 3DY
Tel: 071–583 4748
EdROP aims to develop and monitor learning opportunities in the adult education service for men and women over retirement age in London.

The Scottish Institute of Adult and Continuing Education
30 Rutland Square
Edinburgh EH1 2BW
Tel: 031–229 9166
SIACE is an advisory and consultative body reflecting nationally the interests of organisations, institutions and individuals concerned with the provision of adult education.

The Welsh Joint Education Committee
245 Western Avenue
Cardiff CF5 2YX
Tel: 0222 561231

The Open College
Freepost
Warrington WA2 7BR
Tel: 0925 232899

Skill: National Bureau for Students with Disabilities
336 Brixton Road
London SW9 7AA
Tel: 071–274 0565

University of the Third Age (National Office)
1 Stockwell Green
London SW9 9JF
Tel: 071–737 2541
The University of the Third Age works to increase self-help educational or learning opportunities for retired people. It enables members to share many educational, creative and leisure activities which are organised mainly in small groups that meet regularly, often in each other's homes. A small start-up grant, advice and speakers are available.

The National Extension College
18 Brooklands Avenue
Cambridge CB2 2HN
Tel: 0223 316644
The National Extension College is an education charity providing long-distance learning course for adult learners and resource materials for use in a wide range of educational and training areas. The National Extension College offers a variety of courses to older people. One of its aims is to enable people to have a second chance at education through distance learning—studying in their own home at their own pace. Materials are designed for learning step-by-step (through to GCSE and A level) and courses include basic English, maths, computing, business, languages, engineering, bird-watching, writing, animal management, writing for money—around 80 different subjects.

The National Adult School Organisation
NASO Centre
Gaywood Croft
Cregoe Street
Birmingham B15 2ED
Tel: 021–622 3400
The National Adult School Organisation aims to provide a continuous broad education for life through informal, self-help, friendly discussion groups. Group programmes are usually based on the annual study handbook which provides data about which members may form their opinions at weekly or fortnightly meetings.

Members also have opportunities to meet at local, county and national levels for social and educational events including study weekends, summer schools and international visits.

Workers' Educational Association
17 Victoria Park Square
London E2 9EB
Tel: 081–983 1515

National Institute of Continuing Education
19b de Montfort Street
Leicester LE1 7GE
Tel: 0533 551451

Retirement Education Centre
Bedford College
6 Rothsay Gardens
Bedford MK40 3QB
Tel: 0234 360304

The Open University
PO Box 188
Milton Keynes, MK7 6DH
Tel: 0908 274066
The Open University offers literally hundreds of correspondence courses in numerous subjects: arts, science, technology, maths, etc. The cost varies depending on whether students are pursuing the 'study pack' or a full degree course.

GARDENING

The Royal Horticultural Society
80 Vincent Square
London SW1P 2PE
Tel: 834 4333
The Royal Horticultural Society offers many benefits to RHS members. The £22 (+ £5 enrolment fee) membership fee provides free entry to gardens all over Britain, *The Garden* magazine monthly, special entry to the Chelsea Flower Show and other gardening fairs and free advice on gardening projects and problems.

The National Society of Allotment and Leisure Gardeners Ltd
Odell House
Hunters Road
Corby
Northants NN17 1JE
Tel: 0536 66576
The National Society of Allotment and Leisure Gardeners helps people to enjoy the recreation of gardening and encourages the formation of local associations. It promotes education and publicity and protects allotments for future generations.

The Advisory Committee for Blind Gardeners
Horticultural Therapy
Trunkwell Park
Beech Hill
Reading RG7 2AT
Tel: 0734 884844
The Advisory Committee for Blind Gardeners aims to encourage interest in gardening by visually impaired people and to introduce them to practical ways of overcoming gardening difficulties caused by visual impairment.

DIY and Gardening

People over 60 are entitled to a 10 per cent discount on all DIY and gardening goods at the 260 B & Q stores on Wednesdays. For the local store address, look in the Yellow Pages under DIY stores or ring Readicall on 081–460 4166. Application forms are available in the stores and will require some form of identification that can confirm the applicant's age.

Further Reading
Gardening in Retirement, Isobel Pays (Age Concern England, address page 48), £1.95

SPORTS

The Sports Council positively encourages over-50s to participate in sport and physical recreation and will give advice about where courses, facilities and advice may be found. For further details and publications contact:

The Sports Council
16 Upper Woburn Place
London WC1H 0HA
Tel: 071–388 1277

The Scottish Sports Council
1 Caledonia House
South Gyle
Edinburgh EH12 9DQ
Tel: 031–317 7200

The Sports Council for Northern Ireland
House of Sport
Upper Malone Road
Belfast BT9 5LA
Tel: 0232 381222

The Sports Council for Wales
The National Sports Centre for Wales
Sophie Gardens
Cardiff CF1 9SW
Tel: 0222 397571

The Amateur Swimming Association
Harold Fern House
Derby Square
Loughborough LE11 0AL
Tel: 0509 230431
This Association encourages people of all ages to take up swimming, and has a national award scheme.

The National Association of Swimming Clubs for the Handicapped (NASCH)
The Willows
Mayles Lane
Wickham
Hants PO17 5ND
Tel: 0329 833689
Aims to encourage, develop and promote swimming among handicapped people.

The Scottish Association for the Disabled
c/o Fife Sports Institute
Viewfield Road
Glenrothes KY6 2RA
Tel: 0592 771700
Aims to promote sporting activities for the disabled.

The Veterans' Lawn Tennis Association
26 Marryat Square
Wyfold Road
London SW6 6UA
Tel: 071–386 0484
The VLTA organises competitions, championships and events throughout the UK and internationally. Maintains special clubs and keeps a list of affiliated clubs.

The Ramblers Association
1–5 Wandsworth Road
London SW8 2LN
Tel: 071–582 6878
The Ramblers Association promotes rambling, protects rights of way, campaigns for access to open country and defends the beauty of the countryside. Factsheets (with sae) cost 25p each and include:
Advice and Information for Leaders
Equipment and Safety
Maps and Navigation
Walking in Britain
The Ramblers Association Yearbook and Accommodation Guide (£4.99)

The Senior and Veteran Windsurfers Association (SEAVETS)
34 Nash Grove Lane
Wokingham
Berks RG11 4HD
Tel: 0734 734634

Aims to encourage the not-so-young to take up the sport of windsurfing and participate in national events.

The British Amputee Sports Association
Harvey Road
Aylesbury
Bucks HP21 9PP
Tel: 0296 84848

The Yoga For Health Foundation
Ickwell Bury
Biggleswade
Beds SG18 9EF
Tel: 0767 27271

The British Wheel of Yoga
1 Hamilton Place
Boston Road
Sleaford
Lincs NG34 7ES
Tel: 0529 306851

The British Deaf Sports Council
7a Bridge Street
Otley LS21 1BQ
Tel: 0943 850214

British Ski Club for the Disabled
Berwick Street
Shaftesbury
Dorset SR7 0HQ
Tel: 0747 828515

British Veterans' Athletic Federation
67–71 Goswell Road
London EC1V 7EN
Tel: 071–410 9410
Information about BVAF courses and activities that are available at the nearest leisure centre can be obtained from local libraries.

British Veterans Athletic Sports Foundation
Harvey Road
Stoke Mandeville
Bucks HP21 9PP
Tel: 0296 84848

Central Council of Physical Recreation
Francis House
Francis Street
London SW1P 1DE
Tel: 071–828 3163
As the national association of sport and recreation, the CCPR aims to promote and develop measures to improve sporting opportunities, particularly for the disabled and disadvantaged.

TALKING BOOKS

The National Listening Library
12 Lant Street
London SE1 1QH
Tel: 071–407 9417
The National Listening Library provides a postal service of unabridged talking books and lends a special machine to play these long-playing tapes. The annual subscription is £15 and this covers all postage on cassettes in both directions. Members are provided with a catalogue which contains some 3,000 titles. Membership application forms can be obtained from the NLL, together with a descriptive leaflet. The form requires certification that a member has a disability which makes it difficult for him or her to read a book in the normal way. The visually impaired obtain their talking books from the Royal National Institute for the Blind.

Wireless for the Bedridden Society
159a High Street
Hornchurch
Essex RM11 3YB
Tel: 0708 621101

ARC Section
National TV Licence Records Office
Bristol BS98 1TL
Tel: 0272 230130
The Accommodation for Residential Care (ARC) section of the TV licence authority offers TV licences at a reduced fee to people in strictly defined accommodations. These include physically disabled persons in their own rooms in residential and nursing homes and certain sheltered housing schemes. Details of conditions of eligibility for reductions are available in a leaflet.

Cassette Library of Recorded Books (Calibre)
Aylesbury
Bucks HP22 5XQ
Tel: 0296 432339
Calibre is a lending library of recorded books for the blind and disabled. Its purpose is to provide a free, easy library for anyone who is unable to read printed books.

Free Tape Recorded Library for the Blind
105 Salusbury Road
London NW6 6RH
Tel: 071–624 8844

The Talking Newspaper Association
90 High Street
Heathfield
E. Sussex TH21 8JD
Tel: 0435 866102

The library provides a large range of publications to the blind or partially sighted on cassette.

The Housebound Readers Service
Brompton Library
210 Old Brompton Road
London SW5 0BS
Tel: 071–244 6469

Books for People Who Are Housebound

Age Exchange Theatre Trust
11 Blackheath Village
London SE13 9LA
Tel: 081–318 9105
The Age Exchange Theatre Trust is a reminiscence centre and museum which arranges social activities and theatre productions, education, publishing and health training for the growing national interest in reminiscence and oral history.

Exploring Living Memory
20 Ivybridge Close
London Road
Twickenham TW1 1EA
Tel: 081–892 1870
Exploring Living Memory co-ordinates reminiscence groups in the Greater London area, offers advice and runs workshops.

Reminiscence
Help the Aged
St James Walk
London EC1R 0BE
Tel: 071–253 0253

THE ARTS

The Tibble Trust
25 Fryerning Lane
Ingatestone
Essex CM4 0DD
Tel: 0277 353691
The Tibble Trust runs courses all over the country in conjunction with local authorities in arts and music, aimed at enhancing the quality of life of elderly or handicapped people.

Shape London
1 Thorpe Close
London W10 5LE
Tel: 081–960 9245
Shape is an arts development agency working for the rights of disabled people and other under-represented groups to complete access opportunity and equality at every level of the arts in London. The Shape network extends through England, Scotland and Wales,

with 16 different centres throughout the UK.

ITHACA
Unit 1
St John Fisher
Sandy Lane West
Blackbird Leys
Oxford OX4 5LD
Tel: 0865 714652
ITHACA (part of the Shape network) aims to make the arts available to people who do not normally have access to them in Oxfordshire and Berkshire.

Artability
St James Centre
Quarry Road
Tonbridge Wells TN1 2EY
Tel: 0892 515478
Part of the Shape network, this voluntary organisation was formed to increase opportunities for disabled people to participate actively in creative arts in Kent, Surrey and Sussex.

The Arts Council of Great Britain
14 Great Peter Street
London SW1P 3NQ
Tel: 071–333 0100
Aims to improve the knowledge, understanding and practice of the arts and increase their accessibility to the public.

The Arts Connection
Cumberland Centre
Reginald Road
Portsmouth
Hants PO4 9HN
Tel: 0705 828392
Promotes arts for older and disabled people

Conquest (The Society for Art for the Physically Handicapped)
3 Beverley Place
Ewell
Epsom
Surrey
Tel: 081–393 6102
Conquest encourages adults with physical disabilities to pursue creative art activity in the home, in company and in the community.

The National Association of Drama with the Blind
Pinfold
97 Town Green
Rothley
Leics LE7 7NW
Tel: 0533 302877
Education, instruction and participation in the dramatic arts involving a drawing together of knowledge and skills, and developing drama with visually handicapped people worldwide.

GENERAL INTERESTS

The National Trust
36 Queen Anne's Gate
London SW1H 9AS
Tel: 071–222 9251

The National Trust for Northern Ireland
Rowallane House
Saintfields, Ballynahinch
Co. Down BT24 7LH
Tel: 0238 510721

The National Trust for Scotland
5 Charlotte Square
Edinburgh EH2 4DU
Tel: 031–226 5922
The National Trust preserves historic buildings, gardens, parks, countryside, coastline and historic sites and also offers holiday cottages in England, Wales and Northern Ireland. It publishes a free booklet, *Facilities for Disabled and Visually Handicapped Visitors* and the annual subscription allows free entry into National Trust properties.

Camping for the Disabled
20 Burton Close
Dawley
Telford
Tel: 0743 761889
Camping for the Disabled offers advice to disabled people and their families on camping and caravanning and organises group camps at adopted sites.

British Jigsaw Puzzle Library
8 Heath Terrace
Leamington Spa
Warwicks CV32 5LY
Tel: 0926 311874
The Leamington Spa British Jigsaw Puzzle Library is a postal lending library for jigsaws.

The Older Feminists Network
54 Gordon Road
London N3 1EP
Tel: 081–346 1900
The aim of the Older Feminists Network is to counter the negative stereotypes of older women in society, to challenge the ageism and sexism which older women suffer and to provide contacts, mutual support and the exchange of ideas and information by mobilising the skills and experience of older women in campaigning for change.

NEWSPAPERS AND MAGAZINES

Saga
Saga Publishing Ltd
The Saga Building
Middleburg Square
Folkestone
Kent CT20 1AZ
Tel: 0303 857523

Choice
2 St John's Place
St John's Square
London EC1M 4DE
Tel: 071–490 7070

Yours
Apex House
Oundle Road
Peterborough PE2 9NP
Tel: 0733 555123

Mature Tymes Monthly
25 High Street
Cowbridge
South Glamorgan CF7 7AE
Tel: 0446 775522

Prime of Life
15 Trafalgar Street
Plymouth
Devon PL4 9PE
Tel: 0752 250984

50 Forward
1–2 Ravey Street
London EC2A 4QP
Tel: 071–739 7883

Active Life
Christ Church
Cosway Street
London NW1 5NJ
Tel: 071–262 2622

Grown Ups
45 Station Road
Redhill
Surrey RH1 1QH
Tel: 0737 767213

Civil Service Pensioner
7 The Beeches
Shaw Hill
Melksham
Wilts SN12 8EW
Tel: 0225 702416

Pensioners' Voice
Melling House
14 St Peter Street
Blackburn
Lancs BB2 2HD
Tel: 0254 52606
Newspaper of the organisation which campaigns for a better deal for older people.

OTHER USEFUL ORGANISATIONS AND ADDRESSES

Memories on Video
24 York Gardens
Winterbourne
Bristol BS17 1QT
Tel: 0454 772857
This company will transfer old cine films onto videos.

Memory Makers
1 South Street
Exmouth
Devon EX8 2SX
Tel: 0395 264000
Restores old photographs.

The Oral History Society
Department of Sociology
University of Essex
Wivenhoe Park
Colchester 3SQ
Tel: 0206 873333

Heraldic Times
79–80 Northgate
Canterbury
Kent CT1 1HE
Tel: 0227 462618
How to trace family ancestry.

Instep Dance Promotions
Coppersnere
The Lane
Corston
Bath
Avon BA2 9BA
Videos to learn dance at home.

Holmfirth Wools
Egypt Road
Thornton
Bradford BD13 3RG
Tel: 0274 835365
Mail-order knitting wools.

Embroiderers' Guild
Apartment 41
Hampton Court Palace
East Molesey
Surrey
KT8 9AU
Tel: 081–943 1229

Ehrman Kits Ltd
Lancer Square
London W8 4EP
Tel: 0932 770342
Tapestry by mail.

The British Antique Dealers Association
20 Rutland Gate
London SW7 1BD
Tel: 071–589 4128

British Chess Federation
9a Grand Parade
St Leonard's-on-Sea
East Sussex TN38 0DD
Tel: 0424 442500

British Correspondence Chess Association
86 Mortimer Road
London N1 4LH
Tel: 071–254 7912

British Wireless for the Blind Fund
Gabriel House
34 New Road
Chatham
Kent ME4 4QR
Tel: 0634 832501
Radio-lending agency.

National Listening Library
12 Lant Street
London SE1 1QH
Tel: 407 9417

The Writers Bureau
Freepost BY1743
Manchester M1 1JB
Tel: 0800 262382
Learning to write.

Further Reading
Coming of Age: A Positive Guide to Growing Older, David Hopman (ed), (Hamlyn, 1989), £14.95

Directory for Older People: A Handbook of Information and Opportunities for the Over-55s, Ann Danborough and Derek Kinrade (compilers), (Woodhead-Faulkner, 1989), £17.95

50+ Volunteering—A Guide for Those Working with Volunteers, the 50+ group (Volunteer Centre, 1990), free with sae

Growing Old Disgracefully—New Ideas for Getting the Most Out of Life, The Hen Co-op (Piatkus, 1993), £6.99

Plan Your Retirement—Maximising Your Income as You Give Up Paid Employment, Judith Samson and Sue Thomas (compilers), (Consumer Association, Hodder and Stoughton, 1990), £7.95

twelvechapter twelve

DEATH AND BEREAVEMENT

Arranging and Paying for the Funeral, Administering Your Parents' Estate and Coping with Grief and Loss

THE DEATH OF A PARENT, partner or other close relative or friend is a particularly stressful experience which can be eased somewhat if, in various practical ways, preparations have been made in advance.

In this chapter I look at the various ways in which planning can help people to come to terms and cope more easily with the thought of death, as well as examining the practical arrangements that have to be followed after a death. I also consider the effect of bereavement on people, and some ways of dealing with grief.

PLANNING FOR DEATH

Although death is considered a taboo subject in many families, a great burden can be removed from the family if older people are able to face up to the inevitability of their own passing and make their wishes known. No better illustration of this can be shown than with the writing of a will, as described in Chapter 7.

In addition to a will, it is beneficial to discuss and clarify with your parents their wishes about the way the funeral is to be arranged, the type of service that may be conducted (with even an order of service) and their wishes *vis-à-vis* burial, cremation, etc. Often the survivors will be in a state of shock immediately following a death and, because there is a great deal to do in a short space of time, may not prepare or arrange everything with their normal consideration. For instance, they might arrange a more lavish funeral than they can afford, or even agree to certain types or quantities of flowers or an order of service which, however small an issue it may seem, they may subsequently regret.

A great many of these problems can be anticipated in advance. Openness in this, as in medical matters, will invariably produce a reassuring response as opposed to the uncertainty of silence. However, it is certainly a difficult subject to broach, and you should choose your moment carefully and with sensitivity.

Perhaps you could begin by talking about your own will, and where it is kept. Alternatively you could refer to other people that you may know or have read about who have died without making their wishes known, thus causing considerable difficulty for those left behind. This can lead to a general discussion about your parents' affairs and whether they are in order, whether a will has been made and whether they have any specific wishes that you ought to be aware of. As can be seen later in this chapter, it is also useful to know the name of their doctor and solicitor.

Imminence of Death

If you know one of your parents is dying, it is often difficult to carry on a normal relationship, particularly if that parent is at home with you. However, everyone should make a conscious effort to act calmly and as normally as possible. In such circumstances it is as well to be prepared for the question 'Am I going to die?' or to tell your parent that he or she might not have much longer to live. In either case it will depend upon your relationship with and knowledge of your parent to determine what you should say.

For some people the knowledge that death is imminent is very difficult to come to terms with and might disturb the peace of their last days or weeks. For others it has the opposite effect and allows them time to prepare themselves mentally and spiritually.

The Natural Death Centre

20 Heber Road
London NW2 6AA
Tel: 081–208 2853

The Natural Death Centre is an organisation launched in 1991 which has as its overall aim to help improve the quality of dying. The Centre:

- provides information and support for families looking after a dying person at home
- helps families with information to be able to arrange funerals with or without using undertakers
- publishes information on the best and most helpful undertakers, crematoria and funeral suppliers
- hosts workshops for the general public on 'exploring our own death', as well as meetings and dinner discussions to break the taboo of discussing death and dying. These are all held around the country
- provides bereavement and individual counselling
- assists in the preparation of *A Living Will* (which indicates how much high-tech medical intervention the signatory would want if suffering from a terminal disease)
- issues a Declaration of Rights for the person dying at home.

The Natural Death Centre will send a complete information pack in return for four first-class stamps, and asks for donations if possible from people wanting specialised advice. They will also send details on *The Living Will* in return for two first-class stamps.

The Voluntary Euthanasia Society

13 Prince of Wales Terrace
London W8 5PG
Tel: 071–937 7770

The object of the Society is to make it legal for an adult person, who is suffering severe distress from an incurable illness, to receive medical help to die at his or her own considered request. The Society produces a free leaflet called *The Last Right: The Need for Voluntary Euthanasia.*

Further Reading

The Natural Death Handbook, The Natural Death Centre (eds), (available from the Centre), £10.95 including p & p

This book covers the subjects of improving the quality of living and dying, and includes, among other topics, details of how to care for someone dying at home, how to prepare for dying and a consumers' guide to the best undertakers, crematoria and similar organisations.

Who Dies? An Investigation of Conscious Living and Conscious Dying, Stephene Levine (Gateway Books, The Hollies, Wellow, Bath BA2 8QJ), £7.95

Deathing, An Intelligent Alternative for the Final Moments of Life, Anya Foos-Graber (Airlift, 26 Eden Grove, London N7), £13.50

Both books are recommended by The Natural Death Centre as the best reading on spiritual preparations for dying.

The Living Will—Consent to Treatment at the End of Life (Age Concern and Edward Arnold), £5.99

A working party report available from Age Concern (address page 48), it analyses the potential role and effects of advance directives, and in particular the 'Living Will'.

Coming Home, A Guide to Dying at Home with Dignity, Deborah Duda (Airlift, 26 Eden Grove, London N7), £13.50

Recommended by The Natural Death Centre as the best book on dying at home.

Paying for the Funeral in Advance

It is possible not only to plan the funeral arrangements in advance but also to ensure that there will be adequate money to pay the costs.

After a death, the bereaved family is unlikely to be in a state to wish to enter into commercial negotiations with a funeral director (see below) or concern themselves about whether there is money available for the funeral.

One way of ensuring that there is adequate money is to use a traditional life assurance scheme. Under these, various types of policy and payment can be put together, either by a single lump sum payment, by regular payments for a fixed period or until death, or by a combination of these two options. However, unless the plans allow for an element of inflation-linking of the amount assured under the scheme, it is possible that rising prices may mean that there is insufficient money to meet the full costs of the funeral.

There are also companies that produce similar schemes which are not linked directly to insurance. These may offer a number of plans at varying levels of expense (from as little as £100) which guarantee the actual type of funeral selected to be paid for in advance at the prices prevailing at the date of entering the plan.

The costs covered may include only the bare essentials of the funeral or may meet all the ancillary costs such as cremation fees, a contribution to a minister of religion, and other similar items. This can be an attractive proposition, because not only does it cover the costs of the funeral, it will also mean that the exact requirements of your parent will have been sought and responded to. The selected funeral directors will sign a legally binding contract which guarantees that the selected funeral arrangements will be carried out exactly as and when required, at no further cost.

There is generally no age limit for applicants to these schemes.

Chosen Heritage
Farringdon House
East Grinstead
W. Sussex RH19 1EW
Tel: 0342 312266 or Freephone 0800 525555
Chosen Heritage, which is recommended by Age Concern, offers a choice of guaranteed funeral plans, whereby people can arrange and pay for the service of their choice at today's price. A plan gives peace of mind and spares relatives the anxiety and expense of organising the funeral at the time of bereavement. All payments go into an independent trust fund, with Barclays Bank acting as custodian trustees.

Golden Charter
Crowndale House
1 Ferdinand Place
Camden
London NW1 8EE
Tel: 0800 833 800

Golden Charter, recommended by the Society of Allied and Independent Funeral Directors, provides four types of guaranteed funeral plan. Contact them for more details.

The Co-operative Funeral Bond
Freepost
London SE18 5BR
Tel: 081–808 3837

Dignity in Destiny
Freepost
Manchester M1 8DJ
Tel: 0800 269318

The Funeral Expenses Plan
Royal Life Insurance
Bretton Way
Peterborough PE3 8BQ

Age Concern (address page 48) factsheet (No 27), *Arranging a Funeral*, refers to a number of alternative schemes.

Donation of Body and Organs

Many people wish to donate part or all of their body to the medical profession after death, because they feel it can help others. If you believe that your parents may wish to be donors upon their death, it is important that not only do they complete a donor card (see below) but that you and other immediate close relatives are also aware of their wishes.

You also need to be aware of whether they wish to donate specific organs or their whole body. The reason for this is that, if the circumstances are suitable for a possible donation at the time of death, you will be approached about the donation. However, if your parents have at any time expressed an objection to the removal or use of any organs, and their objection did not changed subsequently, you may not override that objection.

However, despite the constant need for organs, the circumstances under which an organ may be removed for use are very limited—usually if a person dies in an intensive care unit in hospital, where the heart may be kept beating even after brain death. There are certain exceptions; the British Organ Donor Society (BODY) is a voluntary organisation which can offer advice to both donors and their families. They provide a factsheet, *Organ Donation and Transportation*, which gives further details.

The British Organ Donor Society
(BODY)
Balsham
Cambridge CB1 6DL
Tel: 0223 893636 or Freephone 0800 444136

It is possible to donate the whole body, and if your parent is interested in this, you must take immediate action upon death to contact your nearest medical school or, if in London:

The London Anatomy Office
Rockefeller Building
University Street
London WC1E 6JJ
Tel: 071–387 7850
Acceptance by the medical school or Anatomy Office is not automatic and will depend upon a number of factors including the cause of death, the need for a post-mortem and the condition of the body at the time of death.

If a whole body donation is accepted, the body may be kept for up to two years, thus preventing effective funeral arrangements. Once it is released a private ceremony may be arranged or the arrangements may be left to the medical school, who will arrange at their own expense a combined service for several donors at once.

If your parents wish to donate organs or their body, they must complete a *donor card*. These cards are available from a number of public places such as most libraries, post offices and doctor's surgeries. Otherwise, they can be obtained from the following:

Department of Health
Leaflets Department
PO Box 21
Stanmore
Middlesex HA7 1AY
Tel: 071–210 5983

All driving licenses which are now being issued also have a donor section incorporated into the license. It is entirely voluntary as to whether this is completed.

There is always a need for organ donors, whereas there are generally more whole-body donors than are required for training purposes. BODY recommends that a multi-organ donor card should be used, and if it is wished it is possible to insert on this 'Whole Body Donor'. There is no age limit for donors of organs for transplant.

WHAT TO DO AFTER A DEATH

When someone dies there are a great many decisions to be taken and arrangements to be made in generally a short space of time. Bereavement is not an easy experience for anyone and usually results in great personal distress to the people responsible for making the decisions and arrangements.

Basic guidance is given below, together with details of books and leaflets which may be obtained for further detailed advice. Many, such as the Social Security leaflet *What to Do After Death—A Guide to What You Must Do and the Help You Can Get*, provide simple and straightforward explanations of the procedures that are recommended to be followed. In practice, much reliance will be placed upon family and friends to provide advice, as well as on the professionals involved such as doctors, priests and funeral directors.

The Doctor's Certificate

Death at Home
The family doctor, if he or she is able to verify the cause of death, will issue a certificate giving the cause of death. If there is to be a cremation, another certificate must be issued and signed by two doctors who are professionally independent of each other. Your own doctor will help you to find the other signatory.

Death in Hospital
The hospital authorities will issue the 'cause of death' certificate to the local Registration Office.

Unexpected Death
A post-mortem may be required. If there is any doubt about the cause of death, a coroner's inquest may be set up. Also a coroner may be involved under other circumstances, such as where a death occurs within 24 hours of admission to hospital, or while a person is being operated on in hospital, or if the deceased person was getting a War Pension. In these cases, the coroner will then notify the Registrar and issue an order for burial or a cremation certificate, as appropriate.

Registering a Death

The 'cause of death' certificate must be registered within five days (eight in Scotland) unless the death has been referred to a coroner. If the coroner held a post-mortem which established that the death was by natural causes, a Form 100, which is issued by the coroner, must also be provided to the Registrar.

The certificate must be taken to the Registrar of Births and Deaths for the area in which the death has occurred. An address for the Registrar will be known by the local doctor, post office, police or local authority or library, or will be in the telephone directory (under Registration of Births, Deaths and Marriages). The certificate should be taken by a member of the family, or by someone with suffi-cient knowledge to provide the Registrar with the following information:

- the full name of the deceased
- date and place of birth
- (if the deceased was a married woman), her maiden name and the full name of her husband
- (in Scotland) the full names of both parents of the deceased, and the profes-sion of the father of the deceased

The Registrar will want to see either the deceased person's National Health Service number or their Medical Card, which has to be handed in. He or she will then issue two certified copies of the entry in the Death Register (the Death Certificate), as well as a Certificate for Burial or Cremation (known as the Green Form, and which will be required by the funeral director or undertaker) and a Certificate of Registration of Death (Form BD8(rev)) which is for Social Secu-rity purposes only.

Further copies of the Death Certificate can be obtained for a small fee. It is advisable to obtain some as they may be needed for probate purposes or to release money before probate from insurance policies, bank deposits or pension funds.

FUNERAL ARRANGEMENTS

Although there is no obligation to hold any ceremony after a death, there can be immense psychological value in so doing. It is a time when family and friends can openly express and share their sadness and is considered an important and necessary part of the process in continuing life after bereavement.

The final funeral arrangements should not made until you are certain that the death does not have to reported to a coroner, since this may effect the date when the funeral can be held.

If you are uncertain about the wishes of your deceased parent or relative in connection with the funeral, it is advisable to check the will to see if there are any directions therein.

Although it is not strictly necessary, the majority of funerals in the UK are arranged by a funeral director. As the arrangements will be discussed at a time of personal distress, it is advisable to obtain written estimates from at least two funeral directors. Even discussing the possibilities available with more than one person helps clarify what is available and at what cost.

There are a large number of funeral directors in the UK, most of whom provide a 24-hour service. The majority are members of the National Association of Funeral Directors (NAFD), a trade association of 2,200 funeral directors which is governed by a code of practice approved by the Office of Fair Trading.

The most significant features of the code are that the funeral directors must provide a price list upon request together with full information on the services that they can provide, they must provide a basic simple funeral if required and a firm estimate. The basic funeral will include the supply of a coffin or casket (respectively tapered or rectangular), a conductor, bearers and a hearse. A basic funeral will not cover the cost of things which funeral directors are generally responsible for, such as church or cremation fees, flowers, additional following cars at the funeral, embalming or notices in the newspapers.

National Association of Funeral Directors
618 Warwick Road
Solihull
W. Midlands B91 1AA
Tel: 021–711 1343

It is necessary to remember that if there is to be a burial in an existing family grave or vault, the funeral director will need the grave ownership document, called a grave grant, which gives permission to use the grave as a vault. You should know where this is and transfer the ownership to another member of the family after the funeral.

Co-operative Funeral Services
29 Dantzic Street
Manchester
M4 4BA
Tel: 061–832 8152 or Freephone 0800 181818 (24-hour answering service)
The Co-operative Funeral Service is the UK's largest Funeral Director, with branches nationwide. They also provide funeral prepayment plans for which enquiries should be made at their local branch, or by telephoning Chester (0244) 341135 for details.

The Cremation Society of Great Britain
Brecon House
Albion Place
Maidstone
Kent ME14 5DZ
Tel: 0622 688292
The Society publishes a quarterly journal, *Pharos International*, and annually a *Directory of Crematoria* (price £16.50 complete with binder or £12.25 for insert only) which includes statistics, details of crematoria costs and siting and planning of crematoria. It also provides, free of charge, information on all aspects of cremation to all members of the public, organisa-

tions, local authorities and any other interested parties. It issues several publications on the subject of cremation.

Oaktree Funeral Services Ltd
Plantsbrook House
94 The Parade
Sutton Coldfield
W. Midlands B72 1PH
Tel: 021–354 1557

National Association of Bereavement Services
122 Whitechapel High Street
London E1 7PT
Tel: 071–247 0617

It is also possible to arrange a funeral on one's own without the assistance of a funeral director. Although few people are willing to go to the necessary lengths required, it can be a very rewarding and intensely personal experience. A number of books are available to assist in the preparations; a common problem identified by them all is the possibility of buying coffins without reverting to a funeral director. It is possible to make them very inexpensively from veneered chipboard panels. The Natural Death Centre makes reference to the following two sources for coffins:

James Gibson Funeral Directors
Tel: 0204 655869
Makes coffins for £45 including handles

Green Undertakings
Tel: 0272 246248

Further Reading
Funerals: And How to Improve Them, Dr Tony Walter (Hodder & Stoughton, Mill Road, Dunton Green, Sevenoaks, Kent TN13 2YA), £8.99

Undertaken with Love, Jane Spottiswood (Robert Hale, 457 Clerkenwell Green, London EC1R 0HT), £12.95

Both these books are on the subject of DIY funerals, and are recommended by The Natural Death Centre.

Factsheet No 27, *Arranging a Funeral* (Age Concern England, address page 48). This factsheet is concerned with help for those who have to arrange a funeral, or who wish to make plans for their own.

Non-Religious Funerals

There are many people who do not feel comfortable with religion or hold strong humanist views against it. Often for these people a religious service would be hypocritical or would lack sincerity.

It is possible to hold non-religious funerals. These are a dignified alternative to a religious funeral, and can be tailor-made to suit the wishes of the deceased and the mourners. The service is conducted by an officiant. The order of service may include music and readings, with the express intention of remembering and perhaps celebrating the life of the deceased.

The officiants, who are trained, come from a variety of backgrounds; they tend to be men and women who are able to empathise with those experiencing grief and loss.

British Humanist Association
14 Lambs Conduit Passage
London WC1R 4RH
Tel: 071–430 0908 or 0608 652063 for the National Co-ordinator for funeral ceremonies.
The British Humanist Association is the national voice of humanism which is concerned with moral issues from a non-religious viewpoint. It plays an important part in arranging non-religious funerals.

National Secular Society Ltd
702 Holloway Road
London N19 3NL
Tel: 071–272 1266
The National Secular Society is the leading organisation in the free-thought movement, supporting unbelievers in the face of religious privilege. It has a large number of officiants able to conduct non-religious funerals. For further information, please send sae.

South Place Ethical Society
Conway Hall
Red Lion Square
London WC1R 4RL
Tel: 071–242 8032
The Ethical Society is an organisation whose chief objectives are the study and dissemination of ethical principles and the cultivation of a rational and humane way of life.

Further Reading
Funerals without God—A Practical Guide to Non-religious Funerals (British Humanist Association), £3.50 including p & p
   Coping with Death, Leslie Scrase (British Humanist Association), £4 including p & p

Paying for the Funeral

You should ensure that you are able to pay for the funeral before finalising the plans for it. The bank account of the deceased will be frozen, unless it is a joint account. Building societies and life assurance companies will generally pay out a limited sum on the production of the Death Certificate before probate has been proved. They are not bound to do so.

If payment has been arranged before death, no problem will arise. However, if no arrangements have been made it is advisable to check that your parents did not belong to an occupational pension scheme that would pay a lump sum to help with funeral costs. In addition, lump sum payments may be available from the deceased's trade union, professional body or other association.

If you are having problems with paying for the funeral the Social Fund may assist towards the cost of a simple funeral. Further details are provided in Chapter 6. Certain criteria are laid down to determine whether you are eligible for assistance. These are whether you are responsible for arranging the funeral, and whether you or your partner are receiving any of these Social Security benefits:

- Income Support
- Family Credit
- Housing Benefit
- Council Tax Benefit.

A claim should be made to your Social Security office within three months of the death. Any payment received from the Social Fund will have to be paid back from any estate of the person who died.

In addition to the Social Fund, assistance may be sought from the local council or health authority.

BEREAVEMENT

We all expect to experience a death in the family at some stage in our lives. Although it is often inevitable, very few people wish to consider the emotional implications in advance. Even if mentally prepared for a death, it is always a time of sadness; if the death is unexpected it will naturally come as a complete shock and cause severe distress.

Grief is a natural emotion which will invariably follow a bereavement. Often it is mingled with feelings of guilt, anger, frustration, loneliness and despair. Many people find the range of emotions confusing and difficult to cope with, particularly if the bereaved is a partner or parent whose support has been relied on for many years.

Although time is the greatest healer of grief, there are a number of stages to helping overcome it. As the severity of the grief and the ability to cope with it will vary from person to person, there is no instant formula that can be produced to heal the spirit.

To begin with, it is important that those who are grieving learn to accept what has happened. They must also try and continue life as normally as possible, taking care of their health and not foregoing regular meals. Often if someone has been cooking for two or more people for many years there is a tendency to ignore meals when alone.

Every attempt must be made to ensure that there is as little to worry about as possible. Once all the legal and administrative formalities are over, the bereaved will need the support of those close to them. Although there is no universally correct way to act, an openness with the emotions and willingness to talk should be encouraged. Grief cannot be resisted; therefore it is better that the bereaved come to terms with their feelings and accept that it is right and natural to mourn—to be unhappy and express that unhappiness.

There are a number of organisations that are able to help people suffering from grief after bereavement.

Age Concern England
Astral House
1268 London Road
London SW16 4ER
Tel: 081–679 8000
Age Concern has a number of local groups which provide services for elderly people. Some offer bereavement counselling.

CRUSE—Bereavement Care
CRUSE House
126 Sheen Road
Richmond
Surrey TW9 1UR
Tel: 081–940 4818
This national organisation offers help to all bereaved people by providing counselling, advice and information on practical problems and opportunities for social contact. CRUSE has over 170 branches throughout Britain, and also provides a wide range of books and helpful leaflets. Send for a free publications list and details of the nearest branch. If there is no branch nearby, CRUSE offers national membership with counsellors available to answer letters and talk on the telephone. They also have contact lists of other widows and widowers.

The branches offer help through counsellors, who are available to visit, at home or elsewhere, and through regular social meetings, providing the opportunity to meet others and make new friendships.

National Association of Widows/Widows Advisory Trust
54–57 Allison Street
Digbeth
Birmingham B5 5TH
Tel: 021–643 8348
The Association, by way of branches

throughout the UK, runs a service providing friendly support, information and advice to all widows to help them to overcome the many problems they face in society today.

The Compassionate Friends
53 North Street
Bristol BS3 1EN
Tel: 0272 539 639 (24-hour answering service)
The Compassionate Friends is a nationwide self-help group of bereaved parents offering friendship and support to others whose child (of any age, including adult) has died. Support is offered through meetings (one-to-one or in a group), leaflets (a list is available upon request), quarterly newsletter, large postal library and SIBBS (Support in Bereavement for Brothers and Sisters) newsletter. It is a befriending, not a counselling organisation.

Gay Bereavement Project
Vaughan M. Williams Centre
Colindale Hospital
London NW9 5HG
Tel: 081–200 0511
Helpline: 081–455 8894
The Project is designed to help gay men and lesbians in the event of a partner dying. It intends to raise awareness that the death of a lover is as traumatic as that of a spouse.

Other Sources of Help
In addition, the local minister or other religious leader will be experienced in counselling the bereaved and will always be helpful, even if the person seeking help is not a regular churchgoer.

There is also a practical organisation which can assist in preventing a specific type of worry after a death. Housewatch offer a service that will provide live-in security if a house is empty after a family bereavement. They will perform such basic tasks as looking after animals, forwarding mail, dealing with suppliers of essential services and tradesmen and ensuring that the property is maintained in good order and repair. They will also assist with house clearance during the period of probate, if required.

Housewatch Ltd
Little London
Berden
Bishops Stortford
Herts CM23 1BE
Tel: 0279 777412

Further Reading
Bereavement: An Advice Leaflet about the Emotional and Practical Aspects of Dealing with Bereavement (Help the Aged), free

A helpful leaflet covering all aspects of bereavement.

DSS Guide 49, *What to do after Death*

After the Death of Someone Very Close, Caroline Morcom (CRUSE), 80p plus 30p p & p

Written by a CRUSE counsellor, the reader is guided through some of the feelings experienced during the grief of bereavement.

Beyond Grief: A Guide for Recovering from the Death of a Loved One, Carol Staudacher (Souvenir Press; available from Bookpoint Ltd, 39 Milton Trading Estate, Abingdon, Oxfordshire OX14 4TD), £7.95

A detailed book on the problems facing those dealing with the death of a loved one or for those helping others who are grieving.

Secret Flowers: Mourning and the Adaptation of Loss, Mary Jones (The Women's Press, 34 Great Sutton Street, London EC1V 0DX), £2.95

A compassionate book that is written out of the personal experience of the author; it treats the experience of grief and loss after a death as being a positive spiritual experience.

Through Grief: The Bereavement Journey, Elizabeth Collick (Darton, Longman and Todd in association with CRUSE), £3.95 plus 65p p & p

Also available on cassette from CRUSE for £5.50 plus 60p p & p. The cassette is complementary to the book and contains a series of direct personal talks to bereaved persons on a range of topics such as grief, anger, guilt, loneliness and depression. It is intended to bring the emotions of bereavement into the open, thus helping the listeners to a point of reassurance and self-awareness.

FINANCIAL HELP FOR THOSE WHO ARE LEFT

Depending upon the individual circumstances, it may be possible to claim extra Social Security Benefits or Pensions when a member of the family dies.

These include:

- Widow's Payment
  This is a tax-free lump sum paid to a widow if her husband has paid enough NI contributions and either she is under 60 or her deceased husband was not getting Retirement Pension when he died.
- Widowed Mothers Allowance
  This can be claimed if a widow has at least one child for whom she can claim Child Benefit.
- Widow's Pension
  This is paid to a widow with no dependent children who is over the age of 45, but before she is able to claim Retirement Pension.
- Retirement Pension
  If a widow and her deceased husband were receiving Retirement Pension when he died, the widow may be able to use his NI contributions to obtain extra pension.
- War Widow's or Dependant's Pension
  Widows and orphans, near relatives or widowers may be able to claim War Pensions if the deceased died as a result of service in HM Armed Forces.
- Guardian's Allowance
  If someone is entitled to Child Benefit for a child taken into the family as the result of a death, the family can also claim Guardian's Allowance.

Further details of these and other benefits, with details of how to claim, can be found in the following DSS booklets:

D49 *What to Do After a Death*
NP45 *A Guide to Widow's Benefits*
N151 *National Insurance for Widows*

ADMINISTERING THE ESTATE

If There Is a Will

If a will was prepared, the original must be found. Generally it will be kept with the solicitor who assisted in the preparation of the will or with the deceased's bank. Once found, its validity must be ascertained. Consideration must be given to whether the testator had sufficient mental capacity when the will was drawn up and whether the appropriate formalities were complied with.

If there is a will, it is the responsibility of the executors named in it, acting as the deceased's personal representatives, to obtain the Probate Court's authority to carry out its terms. They will then be responsible for administering the estate.

If assets are held in joint names, these may normally be transferred to the survivor merely by producing a copy of the Death Certificate. Otherwise only limited amounts of money will be released to an executor on production of a death certificate by banks and insurance and pension companies. It is then necessary to have the will 'proved' and to produce a 'grant of probate' before any money can be released. An exception to this is if the total amount of money left by the deceased is £5,000 or less; it is then a case of asking the bank or other institutions holding the money what the formalities are; this normally involves only completing a simple form.

If There Is No Will

If no will has been made, the deceased is said to have died intestate and a personal representative, usually a close relative, must administer the estate. The representative must normally need to apply to a probate registry for a 'Grant of Letters of Administration'. Whereas an executor has full legal authority to administer the estate by virtue of the will and needs probate only by way of confirmation, a personal representative in intestacy has no authority unless and until letters of administration are granted.

The distribution of the estate of someone who dies intestate can be complex, especially if it is large and there is a widow or widower and children. It is recommended that professional advice is sought.

Probate and the Duties of the Executor

The main tasks of the executor are:

- to find out what the deceased has left. This involves writing to all the organisations where the deceased had money, and obtaining valuations where necessary
- to ascertain how much inheritance tax will have to be paid, when is it likely to be paid and calculate how the funds will be raised to pay it
- to complete forms required by Probate Registry (see below), including an Inheritance Tax Return for the Inland Revenue
- to appoint a time to visit the Probate Registry to swear the forms
- to visit Probate Registry in person to swear papers
- to pay Inheritance Tax. The demand is normally received two to three weeks after probate is sworn. From March 1993, the first £150,000 of an estate is treated as exempt, with tax at 40 per cent on anything above this threshold. The rates and the threshold change periodically. Inheritance Tax on freehold property and on a business can be paid by instalments but, on all other assets, it must be paid before receiving Grant of Probate. This can create a problem with the timing of releasing funds from the estate, and it may be necessary to obtain a temporary overdraft facility
- to receive Grant of Probate or Letter of Administration. This is normally received four to five weeks after probate is sworn
- to use the Grant of Probate to get hold of assets within the estate (see below)

- to sell property if necessary
- to pay outstanding debts
- to hand over legacies and bequests
- to deal with whatever money/assets are left (the residue)

The forms required by the Probate Registry and available from them are:
PA1 *Probate Application Form*
CAP44 *Return of Assets and Debts*
CAP30 *Schedule of Stocks and Shares*
CAP37 *Schedule of Property*
PA45 *Matrimonial Home Questionnaire*
In addition you will receive a guide to making a personal application for probate (PA2), a list of probate offices (PA3), a table of fees (PA4) and an envelope in which to return the forms.

When the Grant of Probate or Grant of Letters of Administration is received, it should be sent to all the organisations where the deceased held money as listed in form CAP44. With certain types of asset, such as shares, there are special forms to be filled out and procedures to follow, so it is as well to seek help from a professional adviser such as an accountant or bank.

All major towns in England and Wales have district probate registries which should be able to help with any queries; they are not able to give legal advice. Otherwise go to the local Citizens Advice Bureau or contact:

The Personal Application
Department
Principal Registry of the Family Division
Probate Office
Somerset House
Strand
London WC2R 1LP
Tel: 071–936 6938

Other Points to Remember
There may be other practical arrangements to make or refunds due on certain items in the estate.

For example, if the deceased had a car the estate may be due a part refund of insurance premiums. However, this should be kept in place while the car is on the road until it is sold or the ownership and insurance transferred.

The deceased's credit card bills will need to be paid and then the cards cut up and returned to the issuers.

Gas, electricity and telephone companies should be contacted regarding the supply and payment, and the post office told where to redirect mail.

Season tickets and club memberships could be due to refund the estate—check with each issuer.

If your relative lived in a council house or received housing benefit, you should advise the local authority.

Further Reading
How to Sort Out Someone's Will: A Straightforward Guide to Dealing with Probate (Consumers' Association, Castlemead, Gascoyne Way, Hertford, SG14 1LH), £7.95
This book contains a pack listing the main probate registries and local offices, a progress checklist and a checklist of the essential steps to take.
Wills and Probate (Consumers' Association), £9.95
One of the most comprehensive guides on the subject and written for the layman. The book is regularly updated.
What to Do When Someone Dies (Consumers' Association), £9.95
A regularly updated guide to the practical arrangements following a death. Recommended by the Natural Death Centre as the 'best book on red tape surrounding death'.
Factsheet 14, *Probate: Dealing with Someone's Estate* (Age Concern, address page 48). Scottish law differs, therefore Age Concern Scotland (address page 48) issues different factsheets on the subject.
When Someone Dies (leaflet from Money Management Council, PO Box 77, Hertford, Herts SG14 2HW), free

Taxation When Someone Dies

The executor of the estate will normally be responsible for completing an income tax return covering the period from the beginning of the financial year (6 April) up to the date of death. As in a normal tax return, all income and capital gains must be declared. It is a useful exercise to compare the previous return submitted to the Inspector of Taxes to ensure that everything is included. If a copy is not available the Inspector will provide one.

A full year's personal allowances are granted in the year of death. Therefore it is quite common to receive a tax rebate. If tax is due, it must be paid from the estate of the deceased. If the tax return reveals a source of income of which the Inspector was not previously aware, the Inspector is entitled to claim arrears of tax for the previous six years. The executor should therefore satisfy him- or herself that all taxes have been paid before the estate is distributed.

During the period between the death and the distribution of the estate (the administration period), any income that may arise is entered on a tax return by the executor. Income tax is paid at the basic rate. When the income is distributed to the beneficiaries, they are credited with this tax. If they pay higher rate tax, they may be liable to pay more, but if they pay no tax they will be eligible for a refund.

INDEX